JUDAISM AND OTHER FAITHS

Judaism and
Other Faiths

Dan Cohn-Sherbok

Lecturer in Jewish Theology
University of Kent at Canterbury

St. Martin's Press

First published in Great Britain 1994 by
THE MACMILLAN PRESS LTD
Houndmills, Basingstoke, Hampshire RG21 2XS
and London
Companies and representatives
throughout the world

A catalogue record for this book is available from the British Library.

ISBN 0–333–57523–7

Printed in Great Britain by
Ipswich Book Co Ltd
Ipswich, Suffolk

First published in the United States of America 1994 by
Scholarly and Reference Division,
ST. MARTIN'S PRESS, INC.,
175 Fifth Avenue,
New York, N.Y. 10010

ISBN 0–312–10384–0

Library of Congress Cataloging-in-Publication Data
Cohn-Sherbok, Dan.
Judaism and other faiths / Dan Cohn-Sherbok.
p. cm.
Includes bibliographical references.
ISBN 0–312–10384–0
1. Judaism—Relations—History. 2. Religious pluralism—Judaism—
–History. 3. Religious tolerance—Judaism—History. I. Title.
BM534.C64—1994
296.3'872—dc20
                                            93–26260
                                            CIP

For Lavinia, Herod and Dido

Contents

Acknowledgements

In writing this study I would like to acknowledge my indebtedness to a number of important works which have provided information as well as source material: Walter Jacob, *Christianity through Jewish Eyes*. Cincinnati, 1974; Hyam Maccoby, *Judaism on Trial: Jewish–Christian Disputations in the Middle Ages*, London, 1982; Leon Poliakov, *The History of Anti-Semitism*, 2 vols, London, New York, 1965, 1973; David Novak, *Jewish Christian Dialogue*, Oxford, 1989. I would also like to thank Mollie Roots, Justine Clements, Jane Wrench, and Barbara Duce of the Rutherford College Secretarial Office for typing the manuscript.

Introduction

In contemporary society there has been a growing interest in the
world's religions. Within Christian circles a number of theologians
have attempted to formulate a theology of religious pluralism. In
Judaism on the other hand Jewish thinkers have paid scant attention
to this despite the recent developments of Jewish–Christian dialogue and encounter. Despite the contributions of such Jewish
scholars as Louis Jacobs, David Hartman and Norman Solomon
there has not appeared a full-length study of the relationship
between Judaism and other faiths. The purpose of this book is thus
to survey the historical evolution of Jewish thinking about other
religions through the ages, and to formulate a new theological
approach for understanding Judaism in a religiously plural
universe.

The book begins with an examination in Chapter 1 of Christian
reflection about religious pluralism. Some conservative writers have
advanced a traditional form of Exclusivism based on the view that
Christianity constitutes the one, true path to God. Other more liberal
writers however, have criticised the narrowness of this position:
what is currently required, they argue, is a theology of religious
Inclusivism which affirms that God has been active in non-Christian
religions despite the fact that Christ is the definitive revelation of
God. An even more tolerant stance has been advocated by Christian
Pluralists who maintain that the Divine, rather than Christ, is at the
centre of the universe of faiths. Given that there has been no similar
interest in exploring the relationship between Judaism and other
faiths, this theoretical model of Exclusivism, Inclusivism and
Pluralism will be used throughout this book as the theoretical
framework for assessing the Jewish response to other faiths through
the centuries.

Chapter 2 continues this discussion by outlining the Jewish
attitude to other religions in the biblical period. In the Hebrew
Scriptures the Jewish people are depicted as the sole recipients of
God's revelation. Such a view gave rise to the rejection of foreign
gods who were perceived as non-entities. Yet despite the harsh
condemnation of Israelite idolatry by such prophets as Elijah,
pagans were not condemned for their religious practices. Idolatry
was sinful only for the Israelite nation since it was a violation of

1

the Covenant. Here then in the earliest period of history of the Jewish people, there existed a form of Exclusivism – nonetheless there was a recognition that even those who did not acknowledge the God of the Israelites would one day recognize that he is the Lord of history – there is hope then even for pagan nations in the unfolding of God's providential plan. This attitude of tolerance continued into the rabbinic period. According to the rabbis, those who accept the Noahide Laws are acceptable to God; even those who appear to worship idols are admissible as long as the gods they worship are conceived as symbolically pointing to the one, true God. Later this conception of symbolic intermediacy was applied to Christian believers by such scholars as Rabbenu Tam. In his view, Christianity despite appearances is not idolatry. Other writers such as Judah Halevi advanced an even more tolerant form of Jewish Inclusivism – in their opinion Christians as well as Muslims have an important role to play in God's plan for humanity.

Such openness to other faiths was undermined by the terrible events of the Middle Ages. As Chapter 3 explains, throughout Europe Jews were continually massacred for allegedly committing such crimes as murdering Christian children and using their blood for ritual purposes at Passover, defaming the host, blaspheming Christ, and bringing about the Black Plague. Such anti-Jewish sentiment was intensified by a series of Jewish–Christian disputations which took place in the thirteenth and fifteenth centuries. The first of these confrontations took place in Paris in 1240 to ascertain whether the Talmud contains blasphemies against Jesus and Christianity. Although Jewish representatives endeavoured to defend themselves against these charges, the encounter resulted in the condemnation and burning of the Talmud. Two decades later a second disputation took place in Spain; the purpose of this encounter was to convert the Jewish populace. Again, this confrontation caused considerable alarm among the Jewish inhabitants. The third disputation occurred in Tortosa at the beginning of the fifteenth century lasting for nearly two years; the Jewish community was terrified of the outcome and feared for their safety. Hence during these centuries the Jewish population lived in the shadow of a crusading Church, and as a result there was little attempt to formulate a positive assessment of Christianity or of any other faith.

Due to the Christian attempt during the Middle Ages to convert the Jewish population, a large number of Jews embraced Christianity. As Chapter 4 illustrates, this step initiated a dark and bloody period in the history of Jewish–Christian relations: in the fifteenth century the Church instituted a new form of Jewish persecution. Under King Ferdinand and Queen Isabella of Spain, the Inquisition was unleashed upon these new converts (Marranos) to determine if they were loyal to the Christian faith. Throughout the land, tribunals were established to extract confessions from the guilty. Anxious to escape such persecution, many Marranos sought refuge in Portugal where they led a Christian way of life while secretly practising Judaism. During this time of turmoil, many Jews awaited the coming of the Messiah to lead them back to Zion, and in the seventeenth century a number of Marranos and others placed their hope in the false Messiah, Shabbatai Tzevi, who subsequently converted to Islam. Despite this act of apostasy, a number of followers continued to believe in him while embracing the Islamic faith. Later a new Shabbatean sect was founded by Jacob Frank who believed himself to be the incarnation of Shabbatai Tzevi as well as the second person of the Trinity. Thus in the centuries following the disputations of Tortosa, Jewish life underwent considerable religious confusion as Jews struggled to reconcile loyalty to their ancestral faith with pressures for conversion to Christianity as well as Islam.

With the French Revolution, Jewish life radically changed – no longer was Jewry confined to isolated ghettos. As Chapter 5 indicates, the spirit of emancipation freed Jews from their traditional lifestyle and enabled them to enter into Western life and culture. The origins of Jewish thought during this period of change stem from seventeenth-century Holland where Jewish thinkers such as Baruch Spinoza attempted to reevaluate Judaism in the light of current scientific findings. In the next century the Jewish philosopher Moses Mendelssohn argued that all peoples are capable of discerning the Divine through human reason: in his writings such a fusion of universalism together with Jewish particularism constituted a modernist conception of Jewish Inclusivism. Two other liberal thinkers of this period – Joseph Salvador and Abraham Geiger – similarly adopted a sympathetic appreciation of other traditions while at the same time adhering to the belief that Judaism is the superior religion.

Chapter 6 continues this examination of Jewish theologians during the period of the Enlightenment. Pre-eminent among nineteenth-century thinkers the Reform rabbi Samuel Hirsch believed that through the ages Judaism struggled against paganism. In this quest, he argued, Christianity has an important role – nonetheless it is the

Jewish faith which is humanity's ultimate hope. Similarly the Reform rabbi Solomon Formstecher stressed that Judaism is the ultimate form of the religious life even though God's providential plan is furthered by both Christianity and Islam. A third thinker of this period, the Reform rabbi Solomon Ludwig Steinheim also viewed Christianity in much the same light. In contrast with these thinkers however the Jewish philosopher Hermann Cohen was severely critical of Christian theology; yet despite such reservations he pleaded for a better relationship between Christians and Jews. These qualified endorsements of Christianity were later superseded by Claude Montefiore's attempt to portray the Christian faith in the most positive light. According to Montefiore, God revealed himself to the Christian community as well as to the Jewish people – by understanding this disclosure, he stated, it is possible for Jewry to gain further religious insight.

As Chapter 7 demonstrates, a number of Jewish theologians in the modern period have been anxious to explore the origins of Christianity and its development through the centuries. The Central European writer Max Brod, for example, admired Jesus as a Jewish teacher. However despite his positive evaluation of Jesus' life and teaching, he was critical of Pauline theology; in addition, he argued that as the Christian faith evolved, it became corrupted by paganism. In his view, the only hope for humanity is Judaism. By contrast the German Jewish theologian Franz Rosenzweig was preoccupied with theological truth rather than the historical events of the first century. For Rosenzweig paganism does not provide a viable approach to God – Judaism and Christianity on the other hand provide a true path to the Divine. A positive endorsement of Christianity was also propounded by the German Jewish leader Leo Baeck who sought to reclaim Jesus as an authentic Jewish figure. Likewise the German Jewish theologian Martin Buber admired Jesus as a great religious figure. A similar position was advance by the biblical scholar Jacob Klausner who viewed Jesus as a typical Jewish teacher of the period. In Klausner's view Judaism will eventually become the religion for all people, but Jews should acknowledge their debt to Christianity helping to achieve this goal.

In the last fifty years, the Holocaust has had a profound impact on Jewish attitudes towards Christianity. No longer is it possible to look forward optimistically to Jewish–Christian dialogue as envisaged by previous writers. Chapter 8 outlines the views of several contemporary Jewish writers who have continued to explore the relationship between the Jewish and Christian faiths. The German scholar Hans Joachim Schoeps, for example, published a history of Jewish–Christian dialogue in which he claimed that God disclosed himself to both communities in different ways. In a different vein, the American Jewish theologian Richard Rubenstein reformulated his understanding of God as a result of a meeting with the German pastor Heinrich Grüber. An alternative approach to the Holocaust was undertaken by the American theologian Emil Fackenheim who argued that God had disclosed a new commandment at Auschwitz and that both faiths are now obliged to resist contemporary secularism. For two other Jewish theologians – Ignaz Maybaum and Arthur A. Cohen – Christian ideas and motifs have provided the basis for their understanding of God's dealings with the Jewish people during the Nazi era. Hence, during the last few decades a number of Jewish thinkers have explored various aspects of Christian teaching in their quest to understand Jewish existence in a post-Holocaust world.

As Chapter 9 indicates, this survey of Jewish attitudes toward other faiths reveals that Jewish thinkers have generally adopted a tolerant attitude toward the world's religions. In the biblical period the religion of Israel was Exclusivist in orientation, yet other peoples were not condemned for their pagan ways. Moreover, the prophets believed that in the final days the nations of the world would come to recognize Judaism as the one true faith. During the rabbinic period this attitude of tolerance continued to animate Jewish life – according to the rabbis all non-Jews who accept the Noahide laws will be saved. A number of medieval thinkers elaborated similar views and in the modern period there has been a growing recognition of the integrity of other faiths. However in contemporary society the Jewish community needs to adopt an even more open stance toward the world's religions – what is required today is a Copernican shift from Inclusivism to Pluralism in which the Divine – rather than Judaism – is placed at the centre of the universe of faiths. Such Pluralism would enable Jews to affirm the uniqueness of Judaism while urging them to acknowledge the religious validity of other religions. The theology lying behind this transition is based on the distinction between Reality as-it-is-in-itself and the Real as perceived. From such a perspective, the truth claims of all faiths should be regarded as human constructions rather than universal absolutes. The theological implications of such a reorientation of belief are very great: from a

Pluralist standpoint the traditional doctrines of the Jewish faith must be viewed as religious hypotheses rather than certain knowledge. The sweep of Jewish history thus points to a new goal – a global vision of the universe of faiths in which Judaism is perceived as one among many paths to the Divine.

1
The Challenge of Religious Pluralism

In contemporary society with its multiplicity of faiths, there has been an increasing interest in the relationship between the world's religions. Within Judaism only a few thinkers have grappled with the issue of religious pluralism, yet in Christian circles there has been considerable debate about the relationship between the Christian faith and other traditions. A number of conservative Christian theologians have espoused a traditional form of Exclusivism based on the assumption that Christianity contains the one true and final revelation from God. Other thinkers however have criticised such a doctrine for its narrowness. Disenchanted with Exclusivism, they have formulated a modified Christo-centric approach – Inclusivism – which affirms the salvific presence of God in non-Christian religions while still maintaining that Christ is the definitive revelation of God. Although such a model of religious diversity is more liberal than the traditional Exclusivist stance, other Christian theologians have argued for an even greater tolerance of non-Christian religions. On their view, what is now required is a Copernican revolution in which the Divine, rather than Christ, is placed at the centre of the universe of faiths. This reflection about religious diversity can serve as the basis for a theoretical framework for assessing the Jewish response to other faiths over the centuries. As will be seen a number of Jewish writers from ancient times to the present have oscillated between Jewish Exclusivism, Inclusivism and Pluralism, but all have been concerned to make sense of Judaism in the context of other religious traditions.

JUDAISM AND THE WORLD'S RELIGIONS

Recently there has been considerable discussion in Christian circles about the relationship between Christianity and the world's religions.

Traditionally Christians have insisted that those outside the Church cannot be saved. To quote a classic instance of this view, the Council of Florence in the fifteenth century declared that; 'no one remaining outside the Catholic Church, not just pagans but also Jews or heretics or schismatics, can become partakers of eternal life; but they will go to everlasting fire which was prepared for the devil and his angels. Unless before the end of life they are joined to the Church.' (Denzinger, 1952, no.714)

Increasingly, however, for many Christians this view has seemed highly improbable in the light of contact with other faiths. An important document issued by the Catholic Church in 1965 (*Nostra Aetate*), for example, declared that the truth that enlightens every person is reflected also in non-Christian religions. (Hallencruetz, 1977, 37) Never the less, while recognizing the value of other religions, this declaration maintained that the Christian is at the same time under the obligation to preach that Christ is the Way, the Truth, and the Life. (Halbencruetz, 1977, 38)

Similar attitudes have also been adopted by various Christian theologians. Karl Rahner, for example, argued that salvation is open to adherents of other faiths since the devout Muslim, Hindu, Sikh or Jew can be regarded as an anonymous Christian – a status granted to people who have not expressed any desire for it. (Rahner, 1976, Ch.17; 1979, Ch.3) Again, according to Hans Kung, the way is open to all people to attain eternal life in the world's religions. As Kung remarked, 'A man is to be saved within the religion that is made available to him in his historical situation.' In this manner the world's religions are 'the way of salvation, in universal salvation history', the general way of salvation, we can say, for the ordinary people of the world's religions, the more common, the 'ordinary' way of salvation as against which the way of salvation in the Church occurs as something very special and extraordinary. (Neuner, 1967, 52–3)

Other Christian theologians have taken this view further by declaring that Christians must recognize the experience of God in Christ to be but one of many different divine encounters with what has been given to humankind. In this light Christianity should lay no claim to superiority. In the words of John Hick, 'in his infinite fullness and richness of being he exceeds all our human attempts to grasp him in thought...the devout in fact worshipping the one God, but through different, overlapping concepts or mental icons of him.' (Hick, 1980, 48–9)

In contrast with such formulating of a Christian theology of the world's religions, contemporary Jewish thinkers have paid scant attention to the issue of religious pluralism. Though there is an interest in the development of Jewish–Christian dialogue as well as isolated instances of Jewish–Christian–Muslim encounter, the majority of contemporary Jewish writers have not seriously considered the place of Judaism in the context of humanity's religious experience.

A notable exception to this general neglect is a discussion by the Jewish theologian Louis Jacobs in his *A Jewish Theology*. In a chapter entitled 'Judaism and Other Religions', Jacobs stressed that Judaism has always endorsed the view that there is only one God and that the Torah has not been superseded by any other religious tradition. Such a conviction, he believed, compels Jews to declare that the positions of other religions are false if they contradict the Jewish faith. 'Far Eastern faiths are either polytheistic or atheistic. The Christian concept of God is false from the Jewish point of view. Judaism similarly denies that Mohammed received a revelation from God which made him the last of the prophets with the Koran in the place of the Torah.' (Jacobs, 1973, 289). Yet despite such an uncompromising stance, it would be a mistake for Jews to conclude that God has not revealed himself to others or that other religions do not contain any truth. On the contrary, he asserted, the position one should adopt is that there is more truth in Judaism than in other religions.

Another contribution on this topic is by the Israeli Jewish theologian David Hartman. In 'On the Possibilities of Religious Pluralism from a Jewish Point of View' he maintained that the Bible contains two covenants – that of Creation and that of Sinai. The Creation covenant is with all humanity; it is universal and for all generations. The Sinai covenant on the other hand is with Israel – it is a parallel covenant and embraces other communities. On the basis of this scheme, Hartman argued that God has revealed himself to different groups of peoples at various times in history. In a later work, *Conflicting Visions,* he stressed that revelation in history is always fragmentary and incomplete since divine-human encounters cannot exhaust God's plentitude:

Revelation expresses God's willingness to meet human beings in their finitude, in their particular historical and social situation, and to speak to them in their own language. All of these constraints

prevent one from universalizing the significance of the
revelation... Revelation...was not meant to be a source of
absolute, eternal, transcendent truth. Rather, it is God's speaking
to human beings within the limited framework of human
language and history.

(Hartman, 1990, 247–8)

More recently the Orthodox scholar Norman Solomon discussed
the issue of religious pluralism in *Judaism and World Religion*. In a
chapter entitled 'The Plurality of Faiths', he argued that Judaism is
a religion with a mission to all people. In times of persecution, he
stated, this universal goal has been overlooked – yet it has never
disappeared. In bad times it focuses on the messianic task; in
enlightened eras it is expressed in the Jewish quest to work for the
improvement of humanity. In pursuing this goal, the 'covenant of
Noah' (as expressed in the seven Noachide laws) offers a pattern to
seek for others without requiring their conversion to Judaism. What
is demanded instead is faithfulness to the highest principles of
justice and morality. In this context, the dialogue of faiths becomes
an imperative which emerges through our common mission with
other religious traditions. 'In this interfaith encounter,' he wrote,
'we cannot set the bounds of truth; we must listen and try to learn,
grow in experience and forge language, remain open to the world
around us with its myriad peoples and ways, and read and interpret the words of scripture and sage constantly, critically, in the
context of our own age and society.' (Solomon, 1992, 244)

In addition to these initiatives by Conservative and Orthodox
Jewish theologians, I have myself proposed a theory of religious
pluralism in *Issues in Contemporary Judaism*. In a chapter entitled
'Judaism and the Universe of Faiths', I argued that in each and every
generation and to all peoples of the world, God the Divine is
perceived in numerous ways. Thus, neither Judaism, nor for that
matter any other religion, contains a full and definitive understanding of ultimate Reality. Instead, the Ultimate is conceived in
many different forms. In each case these ideas have been conditioned
by such factors as history, language and culture. For these reasons
the religious beliefs are characteristically different in every case.
What is now required, I maintained, is for Jews to free themselves
from an absolutist Judeo-centric position: with the Divine at the
centre of the universe of faiths, Jewish dialogue with other religious
traditions can assume an altogether different and beneficial character.

EXCLUSIVISM

As previously emphasized, the contemporary Jewish reaction to interfaith has been minimal compared with the recent outpouring of Christian responses. Hence it is the writings of modern Christian theologians – rather than Jewish thinkers – which provide a framework for understanding the issue of religious pluralism. For the sake of simplicity, most Christian commentators have outlined three basic responses to other faiths: Exclusivism, Inclusivism and Pluralism. Initially the Christian Exclusivist position (only those who confess Christ and offer their lives to him are saved) was expressed in Acts 4:12 where Peter declared: 'And there is salvation in no one else, for there is no one else, for there is no other name under heaven given among men by which we must be saved.' Again, the Fourth Gospel proclaims: 'I am the way, and the truth, and the life. No one comes to the Father, but by me." (John 14.6).

Such an attitude has been endorsed by the Church through the ages – throughout Christian history, the non-Christian has been viewed as beyond truth and light. Such a claim was institutionalized and enshrined in the axiom of the Catholic Church: *'Extra Ecclesiam nulla salus'* (outside the Church no salvation). Echoing this view, Pope Boniface VIII in the thirteenth century stated that:

> 'We are required by faith to believe and hold that there is one holy, catholic and apostolic Church; we firmly believe it and unreservedly profess it; outside it there is neither salvation nor remission of sins...'

> (Kung, 1967, 26)

In this century similar pronouncements have been made by three important Protestant International Missionary Conferences (at Edinburgh (1910), Jerusalem (1928), and Tambaram (1938)). In addition, this position was the dominant attitude of the World Council of Churches until recently.

On this view, Jesus Christ is the sole criterion by which all religions can be evaluated. In his *Church Dogmatics* the modern Protestant theologian Karl Barth stated an extreme form of this Exclusivist theory. For Barth, the revelation of God in Jesus Christ as attested in Scripture is the only criterion in the sphere of religion. Apart from this revelation, any attempt to know God is an activity of unbelief. Revelation, he asserted, is the self-offering of God on behalf of humanity. The divine initiative is all important: 'Revelation is God's sovereign action on man or it is not revelation' (Barth, 1956, 295). On this view, the Christian gospel belongs with revelation whereas other faiths are simply the product of 'religion'. Thus he concluded:

> At the end of the road we have to tread there is, of course, the promise to those who accept God's judgement, who let themselves be led beyond their unbelief. There is faith in this promise, and, in this faith, the presence and reality of the grace of God, which of course, differentiates our religion, the Christian, from all others as the true religion.
>
> (Barth, 1956, 327)

Another modern proponent of Christian Exclusivism is Emil Brunner who like Barth insisted on the absolute sovereignty of God. According to Brunner, other faiths fall short of God's truth. 'From the standpoint of Jesus Christ,' he wrote, 'the non-Christian religions seem like stammering words from some half-forgotten saying: none of them is without a breath of the Holy, and yet none of them is the Holy. None of them is without its impressive truth, and yet none of them is the truth; for their Truth is Jesus Christ.' (Brunner, 1947, 262). For Brunner, it is Christ who serves as the yardstick for evaluating all other faiths:

> Jesus Christ is both the Fulfilment of all religion and the Judgement on all religion. As the Fulfiller, He is the Truth which these religions seek in vain. There is no phenomenon in the history of religion that does not point toward Him…He is also the Judgement on all religion. Viewed in this light, all religious systems appear untrue, unbelieving and indeed godless.
>
> (Brunner, 1947, 270)

Although Christian Exclusivism has been the dominant approach of the Church for millennia, there are a number of important criticisms that have been levelled at this doctrine. First, such a view arguably fails to take seriously God's concern for all humanity: it makes no sense to believe that a God of infinite love, mercy and justice would condemn the majority of human beings to perdition, most of whom had never even heard of Jesus. Such a God would be an arrogant and malevolent tyrant rather than a loving father of all humanity. As the Catholic theologian Gavin Da Costa has remarked: 'The simple historical fact that most of humankind has never encountered the gospel, coupled with the theological doctrine of a God of universal love, begins to undermine a rigorous Exclusivist position' (Da Costa, 1992, 34).

Another objection to Exclusivism concerns the notion of salvific grace. Even among many Christians who believe that God discloses himself unreservedly in Christ, it is historically and theologically implausible to assert that saving grace is limited only to those who submit to Christ. According to these critics, since Christians through the ages have maintained that God initially revealed himself to the Jewish people and acted on their behalf, it is inconsistent to think that he reveals himself only in Christ. Indeed, the second century theologian Marcion who wished to exclude the Hebrew Scriptures from the canon of holy writings was condemned as a heretic. Thus, the belief that God has acted salvifically on behalf of humanity should be seen as a central tenet of the Christian faith.

A third criticism concerns the Exclusivist's denial of biblical evidence regarding the ways in which Christian faith can be enriched by integrating insights from outside the tradition. In Acts 10 for example Peter confronted the gentile pagan Cornelius; through his conversion Cornelius brought to the Church a new understanding about Christ which was drawn from his background and cultural heritage. Translated to the present, such enrichment can take place when the Church confronts members of other religious traditions – through this encounter the Christian is able to gain fresh insight into his own faith. Such listening and learning presuppose an attitude of openness and receptivity – a dialogical stance diametrically opposed to the Exclusivist position of condescension and condemnation of other paths to God.

A further criticism of Exclusivism is related to the rejection (particularly in the writings of Karl Barth) of any kind of criteria or reasoning derived from areas of knowledge in the theological realm. Rejecting such a stance, a number of contemporary Christians have strenuously defended the role of human reason in the religious sphere. Today many Christians simply refuse to accept Barth's distinction between 'revelation' and 'religion'. Rather than rejecting the insights of religious enquiry, they insist that human reason and investigation have a legitimate role in the spiritual quest. In this respect the Anglican theologian Alan Race has remarked that 'as soon as one allows the normal means of human enquiry and reasoning a role in theological formulation, then one is open to the finite and the historical. It then becomes imperative for the theologian to account for the place of Christianity in the light of the total religious history of the world...He will need to reckon with the fact that religion and culture are so inextricably linked that religious truth is always 'conditioned' knowledge.' (Race, 1983, 28–9).

A final criticism of Exclusivism concerns its unwillingness to recognize the importance of human investigation into the origins of the biblical text. Historical studies have increasingly revealed that the biblical text itself is the product of human reflection – both the Hebrew Scriptures and the New Testament reflect the social, economic and cultural conditions of the time in which they were written. On this view the biblical material did not emerge *ex nihilo* through a single act of divine disclosure – rather the entire canon of Scripture evolved through history. Critics of Exclusivism argue that it is therefore an error to believe that these documents are sacrosanct and immune from human interpretation and error. This new understanding of the Bible calls for a reversal of Christian commitment – no longer is it appropriate for Christians to assert *a priori* that Christ is the supreme embodiment of God's revelation. Instead what is now required is for Christians to lay bare the intentions of the biblical authors and the cultural conditions under which they interpreted God's action in the world. For many Christians then Exclusivism provides no answer to the challenge of religious pluralism in modern society – what is now required is a new theory to explain the relationship between Christianity and other faiths.

INCLUSIVISM

A number of Christians who are disenchanted with Exclusivism have espoused a modified Christo-centric approach which affirms the salvific presence of God in non-Christian religions while still maintaining that Christ is the definitive revelation of God. Arguably such a view is rooted in the New Testament. In the Acts of the Apostles, Peter declared: 'Truly I perceive that God shows no partiality, but in every nation any one who fears him and does what is right is acceptable to him' (Acts 10:35). At Lystra, Paul and Barnabas echoed the same conviction: 'In past generations he allowed all the nations to walk in their own ways; yet he did not leave himself without witnesses (Acts 14:16f). Again, in Paul's speech on the Areopagus, he appeared to recognize the authenticity of the Greeks' worship of an unknown God; in this way he included the spiritual life of the Greeks in the worship of the one true God. The Gospel of Luke also appears to suggest that since the providential ordering of human affairs applies not only to the Jewish community since Abraham but also extends back to the creation of Adam (Luke 3:38), all human history is under God's control.

In the second and third centuries these Inclusivist reflections were elaborated in the logos theology of the Church. Justin Martyr, for example, wrote:

> It is our belief that those men who strive to do the good which is enjoined on us have a share in God; according to our traditional belief they will by God's grace share his dwelling. And it is our conviction that this holds good in principle for all men...Christ is the divine Word in whom the whole human race share, and those who live according to the light of their knowledge are Christians, even if they are considered as being godless (1 Apology 46:1–4).

In the modern period such insights have been developed particularly by Roman Catholics, and have been expressed in various Vatican II documents. Thus *The Declaration on the Relation of the Church to Non-Christian Religions* proclaims:

> The Catholic Church rejects nothing of what is true and holy in these religions. She has a high regard for the manner of life and conduct, the precepts and doctrines which, although differing in many ways from her own teaching, nevertheless often reflect a ray of that truth which enlightens all men.
>
> (Race, 1983, 44)

Unlike Catholic decrees of the past, the Catholic Church has now come to accept that salvation is open to others outside Christendom. Hence *The Dogmatic Constitution on the Church* states:

> Those who, through no fault of their own, do not know the Gospel of Christ or his Church, but who nevertheless seek God with a sincere heart, and, moved by grace, try in their actions to

do his will as they know it through the dictates of their conscience
– those too may achieve eternal salvation. (Race, 1983, 44).

A number of modern Catholic theologians have similarly espoused
an Inclusivist position in line with these official declarations.
Prominent among these writers is the German theologian Karl
Rahner who, in an address entitled 'Christians and the Non-
Christian Religions' proposed several theses which he believed
should be embodied in a Christian theology of religion. First, he
stated that; 'Christianity understands itself as the absolute religion,
intended for all men, which cannot recognize any other religion
beside itself as of equal right.' (Rahner, 1966, p. 118). Yet for Rahner
this conviction does not limit salvation to those who have affirmed
their faith in Jesus Christ. Rather, he believed that non-Christian
religions can be authentic witnesses to God's activity in the world:

> A non-Christian religion…does not merely contain elements of a
> natural knowledge of God, elements, moreover, mixed up with
> human depravity… It contains also supernatural elements
> arising out of the grace which is given…on account of Christ.
>
> (Rahner, 1966, 121)

Since non-Christian religions are legitimate parts of God's plan of
salvation, Rahner argued that non-Christians can be regarded as
anonymous Christians:

> Christianity does not simply confront the members of an extra-
> Christian religion as a mere non-Christian but as someone who
> can and must already be regarded in this or that respect as an
> anonymous Christian.
>
> (Rahner, 1966, 131)

Although not all Christian Inclusivists would accept this notion of
an anonymous Christian, there would be a general acceptance of
Rahner's Christo-centric vision embracing the world's faiths: both
Catholic and Protestant Inclusivists affirm that God's activity is
manifest in all religions even though Christ is the authoritative and
final disclosure of the Divine.

Although Christian Inclusivism has won many adherents, critics
have made serious objections to this interpretation of Christianity
and the world's faiths. The first objection concerns Inclusivism's

affirmation of two seemingly incompatible convictions: the belief in the universal will of God to save, and the affirmation that God has definitively revealed himself in Christ. Those opposed to this doctrine stress that such a position is internally incoherent – if God is concerned with the fate of all humanity, how could final salvation only be provided through faith in Christ? Because of this deficiency the Inclusivist model presents an insurmountable stumbling block to fruitful interfaith dialogue. Citing the words of a missionary theologian who espoused a form of Inclusivism in his dealing with adherents of African religions, the Catholic theologian Paul Knitter emphasized the insuperable problems evoked by such an approach. As the missionary himself confessed:

> By positing the absoluteness of Jesus Christ and of God's Revelation in him…we are still envisaging the other religions from within the absoluteness of Christianity; fundamentally the other religion is none the less disqualified. And, in every fibre of its being, it refuses to be disqualified. If Christianity (because of Christ) is the definitive truth, the absoluteness of God's revelation to mankind, it only remains for the other religions to convert to Christianity…What we have in fact, is a dialogue between the elephant and the mouse.
>
> (Knitter, 1985, 142)

A second problem is related to the conception of an anonymous Christian. For non-Christians the idea that adherents of other faiths are (despite their own self-understanding) anonymous Christians is both incomprehensible and offensive: Jews, Muslims, Hindus, Buddhists, and others would reel in horror at being depicted in this way. For the Christian to regard his own faith as definitive and relegate members of other traditions to the periphery of true belief while simultaneously labelling them as anonymously Christian is profoundly disrespectful. Many Christians who are disenchanted with this Inclusivist interpretation of religious pluralism seek a theory which does not impose Christianity on the adherents of other faiths.

For these writers the Inclusivist stance has prejudged the issue of religious truth – what is required instead is a new theory which will provide a framework for listening to and respecting the theological truths of other religions without subjecting them to a Christo-centric test.

PLURALISM

Those Christians espousing Pluralism have argued for an even
greater tolerance of non-Christian religions. The Pluralist criticism
of Exclusivism is summarized by a Buddhist parable turned into a
poem by John Saxe:

> It was six men of Hindostan,
> To Learning much inclined,
> Who went to see the Elephant,
> (Though all of them were blind):
> That each by observation
> Might satisfy his mind.
>
> The first approached the Elephant
> And happening to fall
> Against his broad and sturdy side,
> At once began to brawl:
> 'Bless me, it seems the Elephant
> Is very like a wall.'
>
> The second, feeling of his tusk,
> Cried, 'Ho! what have we here
> So very round and smooth and sharp?
> This wonder of an Elephant
> Is very like a spear.'
>
> The third approached the animal,
> And happening to take
> The squirming trunk within his hands,
> Then boldly up and spake:
> 'I see,' quote he, 'The Elephant
> Is very like a snake.'
>
> And so these men of Hindostan
> Disputed loud and long,
> Each in his own opinion
> Exceeding stiff and strong,
> Though each was partly in the right
> And all were in the wrong.

(Da Costa, 1992, 35–6)

From a Pluralist perspective, Exclusivists are like these blind men and fail to perceive that religious truth is greater than their own religious perceptions.

Prominent among Christian Pluralists is the English philosopher of religion John Hick. In *God and the Universe of Faiths*, he asked: 'Can we...accept the conclusion that the God of Love who seeks to save all mankind has nevertheless ordained that men must be saved in such a way that only a small minority can in fact receive this salvation? (Hick, 1977, 122). For Hick such a situation is impossible. Rather, he maintained, Christians should view the Christian faith as simply one path among many:

> May it not be that the different concepts of God, as Jahweh, Allah, Krishna, Param Atma, Holy Trinity, and so on...are all images of the divine, each expressing some aspect or range of aspects and yet none by itself fully and exhaustively corresponds to the infinite nature of ultimate reality?
>
> (Hick, 1977, 36)

According to Hick what is required is a Copernican revolution in theology which replaces Christo-centrism with a God-centred conception of religious truth. 'It demands', he wrote, 'a paradigm shift from a Christianity-centred or Jesus-centred to a God-centred model of the universe of faiths. One then sees the great world religions as different human responses to the one divine reality, embodying different perceptions which have been formed in different historical and cultural circumstances.' (Hick, 1973, 131).

Similarly the Catholic theologian Raimundo Panikaar has endorsed a new map of world religions. For Panikaar, the mystery within all religions is both more than and yet has its being within the diverse experiences and beliefs of the worlds' religions: 'It is not simply that there are different ways of leading to the peak, but that the summit itself would collapse if all the paths disappeared.' (Panikaar, 1981, 23). Such a division of the universe of faiths implies that no religion can claim final or absolute authority.

A similar position has been advanced by Stanley Samaratha. God, he argued, is the Mysterious Other: 'The Other relativizes everything else. In fact, the willingness to accept such relativization is probably the only real guarantee that one has encountered the Other as ultimately real.' (Samaratha, 1982, 151–3).

By relativizing all religious figures and revelation, Samaratha did not intend to deny their necessity or reduce them to a common denominator. The Mysterious Other must confront humanity though no particular manifestation is universally valid. A particular religion such as Christianity can claim to be decisive for some people, but no religion is justified in claiming that it is decisive for all.

Again, the Catholic theologian Paul Knitter argued that the theocentric model is a valid reinterpretation of Christian tradition and experience. Jesus should not be understood as God's complete revelation – Exclusivist language in the New Testament should be seen as essentially confessional in nature. Such Christological language, he asserted, is much like the language a husband would use of his wife: 'You are the most wonderful woman in the world', and so on. In the context of a marital relationship these claims are true, but only as an expression of love. Similarly it is possible for Christians to express their dedication to Jesus without adopting an absolutist position. Utilizing the analogy of marriage, Knitter wrote: 'The deeper the commitment to one's spouse and the more secure the marriage relationship, the more one will be able to appreciate the truth and beauty of others. Therefore not only does commitment to Jesus include openness to others, but the greater the commitment to him, the greater will be one's openness to others.' (Knitter, 1985, 201–2).

MODELS OF JUDAISM AND THE WORLD'S RELIGIONS

Following these three models that have been proposed by Christian theologians, it is possible to formulate a framework for assessing Jewish responses to other religious traditions through the ages.

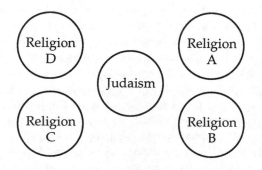

Figure 1.1   Jewish Exclusivism

According to the first model – Exclusivism – Judaism would be at the centre of the universe of faiths. Such a view can be presented diagrammatically, as in Figure 1.1.

On this view Judaism is absolutely true – its source is God. At Mt. Sinai God revealed to Moses his holy Torah. It is the bedrock of certainty which is the mainstay of the Jewish faith. Sinaitic revelation is seen as a unique divine act which provides a secure foundation for the religious traditions of Israel. It is from the biblical account that we learn of God's true nature, his dealings with his chosen people, and the promise of the world to come. In this fashion the Written Torah as well as the rabbinic interpretations of Scripture serve as the yardstick for evaluating the truth claims of other religions.

The significant feature of this model is that it excludes the possibility of God revealing himself to others. It assumes that throughout the history of the world, people have mistakenly believed that they have had an encounter with the Divine, but in fact God only made himself known to the Jews. This accounts for the wide diversity and contradictory character of religious beliefs among the religions of the world. As to those religions which have ideas similar to what is found in Judaism, this concurrence is not due to God's intervention. Rather, the adherents of these religions would have arrived – possibly through the aid of human reason – at religious conceptions which simply happen to be true and therefore conform to what is found in the Jewish faith. Thus, for example, the Muslim belief in one God who is eternal, omniscient, omnipotent and all-good is true, not because God revealed himself to Muhammad, but simply because it coincidentally corresponds with Judaism's understanding. Similarly, Christians would be viewed as coincidentally correct in their adherence to monotheism, but misguided in terms of their conception of the Trinity. On the other hand, polytheistic religions, such as the religious systems of the ancient Near East and the Greek and Roman religions, are utterly fallacious. In all these cases the criterion of true belief is the content of the Jewish religion as revealed exclusively to the people of Israel.

Through such a model is consonant with the attitude of many Jews in the past, it arguably suffers from a very serious theological defect. If God is the providential Lord of history, it is difficult indeed to understand why he would have hidden his presence and withheld his revelation from humanity – except for the Jews. To allow people from the beginning of human history to wallow in

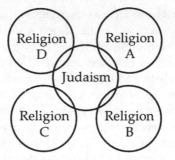

Figure 1.2   Jewish Inclusivism

darkness and ignorance, weighed down by false notions of divine reality is hardly what one would expect from a loving, compassionate and caring God. Rather, while it is true that traditional Judaism maintains that in the Hereafter all the nations of the earth will come to know God's true nature, this does not at all explain why God would have refrained from disclosing himself to the mass of humanity in this life on earth.

To deal with these criticisms, an Inclusivist model – similar to Christian Inclusivism – would assume that God revealed himself not only to the Jews but to others as well. This model can be represented as in Figure 1.2.

Here Judaism would still remain at the centre of faiths, encircled by other religions, but the significant difference between this model and the previous one concerns the role of revelation. Here, non-Jewish religions would be regarded as true, not simply because adherents happened to have similar ideas to what is found in Judaism, but because of a real encounter with the Divine. Judaism would on this view be regarded as ultimately true; its doctrines would serve as a basis for testing the validity of all alleged revelations.

Thus it would be a mistake on this view to think that because a particular religion, such as Theravada Buddhism, has doctrines that directly contradict Jewish theology, God did not reveal himself to the peoples of the Indian continent. On the contrary, it is likely he did, but because of social, cultural, and historical circumstances, this encounter was misunderstood or filtered through human interpretation in such a way that it became confused and distorted. On this account God would have manifested his general concern for humanity throughout history as well as his particular love for his chosen people.

The advantage of this second model is that it not only takes seriously God's love, but it also comes to terms with the human spiritual quest. This is particularly important in the light of the increasing knowledge of religious cultures. Unlike the biblical writers or the ancient rabbis, Jews know more today about Christianity, Islam and the religions of the East; the comparative study of religions has provided insights into the great riches of the religious faiths of the past. In the modern world it is short-sighted to dismiss these traditions as having no religious integrity. What is much more plausible is that in each stream of religious life there have been great mystics, teachers and theologians who have in various ways experienced God's revelation and presence.

This second model preserves the centrality of the Jewish faith while giving credence to the claims of the followers of other religions who have experienced the Divine. None the less, it is questionable whether this picture of the universe of faiths goes far enough. Arguably even this modern approach to the religions of the world does not do full justice to God's nature as a loving father who truly cares for all his creation. On this second model, it is the Jewish people who really matter. They are the ones who have received the full and ultimate disclosure of his revelation; other faiths have only a partial and incomplete view and are pale reflections by comparison. What is missing from even this more tolerant concern is an adequate recognition of God's providential love and concern for all humanity.

To meet these difficulties, it is possible to pose a Jewish Pluralist model similar to what has been espoused by Christian theologians. On such a view, what is far more likely is that in each and every generation and to all peoples of the world, the Divine is considered in distinctly different ways. Thus, neither Judaism nor any other religion contains an absolute and universally valid conception of the Divine. Rather in each case, the view of Ultimate Reality is conditioned by such factors as history, climate, language and culture. For these reasons the doctrine of Divine Reality is characteristically different in every case.

Such a conception of the Ultimate serves as the basis for a Pluralistic model in which the Divine, rather than the Jewish tradition, is at the centre. Judaism, like other religious faiths, encircles the Divine intersecting only at those points at which the nature of

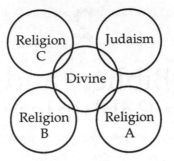

Figure 1.3 Jewish Puralism

divine Reality is truly reflected (see Figure 1.3).

The advantage of this vision of Judaism in the context of the world's religions is that it is arguably theologically more coherent with the Jewish understanding of God as the Lord of creation, and it also paves the way for interfaith encounter on the deepest levels. Already Jews work together with members of other faiths on common projects of fellowship and charity. Yet such a model emphasizes that Jews need to free themselves from an absolutist Judeo-centric position; on this basis the way would be open for interfaith encounter of the most profound kind. With the Divine at the centre of the universe of faiths, Jewish dialogue with other religious traditions would assume an altogether different and beneficial character.

These three models then – Jewish Exclusivism, Inclusivism, and Pluralism – can serve as the theoretical basis for examining the various ways in which Judaism from ancient times to the present has regarded other faiths. As will be seen, attitudes have oscillated between these three approaches depending on the historical, social and cultural setting. Yet, despite the diversity of opinions, a number of Jewish writers through the ages have been concerned to see their own tradition in a wider religious perspective.

2

Biblical and
Early Rabbinic Views

In the Hebrew Scriptures, the Jews are presented as God's chosen people; they alone are the recipients of his true revelation. This conviction led to the renunciation of foreign deities and the prescriptions against idolatry. According to the biblical writers, the gods of other peoples are non-entities. Yet, foreign nations were not condemned for their pagan ways. Idolatry was sinful only for the Jewish people. Here then in the Bible is a mildly tolerant form of Jewish Exclusivism. The religion of the Jews is presented as the one true faith, yet there is no harsh condemnation of idolatry. In addition, the prophets foretold that at the end of days, all people will recognize that the God of Israel is the Lord of history. Thus there is hope even for pagan peoples in the unfolding of God's scheme of salvation. Rabbinic teaching about non-Jews continued this tradition of tolerance: those who follow the Noahide Laws (given originally to Adam and Noah) are viewed as acceptable to God. Even those who engage in seemingly polytheistic practices are admissible as long as the gods they worship are conceived as symbolically pointing to the one true God. In the writings of medieval thinkers such as Rabbenu Tam, this earlier rabbinic conception of symbolic intermediacy was applied to Christian believers: in the view of these scholars Christianity is not idolatry. Some writers such as Judah Halevi formulated an even more tolerant form of Jewish Inclusivism. In their view, Christians as well as Muslims have a positive role in God's plan for humanity: as monotheistic faiths they can spread the message of monotheism to the nations and encourage them to adhere to the Noahide covenant.

THE BIBLE AND IDOLATRY

In the history of ancient Israel the first instance of idolatry occurred after the theophany at Mount Sinai. The Book of Exodus records

that in their despair the people of Israel worshipped a golden calf
constructed by Aaron:

> When the people saw that Moses delayed to come down from the
> mountain, the people gathered themselves together to Aaron, and
> said to him, 'Up, make us gods, who shall go before us; as for this
> Moses, the man who brought us up out of the land of Egypt, we
> do not know what has become of him.' And Aaron said to them,
> 'Take off the rings of gold which are in the ears of your wives,
> your sons, and your daughters, and bring them to me'...And he
> received the gold at their hand, and fashioned it with a graving
> tool, and made a molten calf: and they said, 'These are your gods,
> O Israel, who brought you up out of the land of Egypt!
>
> (Exodus 32:1–4)

When God observed that his chosen people had abandoned him,
his fury blazed forth, and he determined to destroy them – it was
only because of Moses' intervention that the nation was saved
(Exodus 32:11–14). Yet despite such an intervention, when Moses
descended from the mountain top he was enraged and hurled the
tablets he had hewn. He took the calf, burned it, ground it, strewed
it upon the water, and made the people drink it. Then he
commanded the Levites to slay all those who did not accept the
God of Israel (Exodus 32:26–28).

To prevent further lapses, God commanded that the children of
Israel refrain from making any graven images. Thus the Decalogue
proclaims:

> I am the Lord your God, who brought you up of the land of
> Egypt, out of the house of bondage. You shall have no other gods
> before me. You shall not make for yourself a graven image, or
> any likeness that is on the earth beneath, or that is in the water
> under the earth; you shall not bow down to them or serve them;
> for I the Lord your God am a jealous God.

In this regard God decreed that the Canaanites were not to be
tolerated because they would 'cause you to sin against me for you
will serve their gods that this be a snare to you' (Exodus 23:33).
Such concern about Canaanite practices was the basis of the
prohibition of marriages with them (Exodus 34:16); this restriction
was subsequently extended to other pagan peoples when in I Kings

Solomon's downfall was attributed to the idolatrous practices of his foreign wives who 'turned his heart'. (I Kings 11:3–4).

Despite such prohibitions, idolatry continued to flourish, and in the northern kingdom Jeroboam I encouraged a mixture of Canaanite and Israelite religions. Subsequently King Ahab continued these idolatrous practices, incurring the condemnation of Scripture: 'And Ahab the son of Omri did evil in the sight of the Lord more than all that were before him' (I Kings 15:30). Such idolatry was encouraged by his wife Jezebel who wanted Baal to become the god of Israel. To combat this threat, the prophet Elijah was determined to prove the God of Israel was supreme. Thus he challenged 450 prophets of Baal and 400 prophets of Asherah to a contest on Mount Carmel, near Phonician territory. There he and the Canaanite prophets prepared sacrifices and prayed to their respective gods to send fire from heaven to ignite the offerings. Although the prophets of Baal and Asherah cried aloud in ecstatic frenzy and cut themselves with swords, no answer was forthcoming. But Elijah's supplication was successful:

> The fire of the Lord fell, and consumed the burnt offering, and the wood, and the stones, and the dust, and licked up the water that was in the trench. And when all the people saw it, they fell on their faces; and they said, 'The Lord, he is God; the Lord, he is God.'
>
> (I Kings 18:38–9)

As a punishment Elijah had the prophets of Baal rounded up, and he killed them at the brook Kishon.

Repeatedly throughout Scripture the idolatrous ways of surrounding peoples were condemned. In the Book of Psalms for example the gods of these nations are referred to as *Elilim* (non-gods). Yet such denigration did not imply that the ancient Israelites should attempt to enlighten foreign peoples. God's concern was with his chosen people – the Israelites were not to stray from worshipping the one true God. Referring to the incident of the golden calf, the sixth century prophet Jeremiah declared that in the desert the people had committed two sins: they had forsaken God and built an idol to take his place:

> For my people have committed two evils; they have forsaken me, the fountain of living waters, and hewed out cisterns for themselves, broken cisterns, that can hold no water.
>
> (Jeremiah 2:13)

According to Jeremiah, for the Jewish people idolatry is both immoral and foolish. Thus, he advised the exiles in Babylonia how to respond to those who urge them to worship idols:

> Thus shall you say to them: 'The gods who did not make the heavens and the earth shall perish from the earth and from under the heavens...every man is stupid and without knowledge; every goldsmith is put to shame by his idols; for his images are false, and there is no breath in them. They are worthless, a work of delusion.'
>
> (Jeremiah 10:11, 14–15)

Despite such denunciation of pagan beliefs, idolatry was viewed as sinful only for Israel. The prophets did not condemned foreign peoples for their misguided ways. The nations of the world are not to be rebuked for their practices since they are not included within the divine covenant. When they are rebuked it is because of their sinfulness rather than their idolatry. Hence when the eighth century prophet Amos criticized Damascus, Gaza, Tyre, Edom, Amon and Moab, it was because of their treachery (Amos 1:33).

None the less Scripture envisages a time when all peoples will come to recognize that the God of Israel is the Lord of all creation. At that time all peoples will say: 'Come, let us go up to the mountain of the Lord, to the house of the God of Jacob; that he may teach us his ways and that we may walk in his paths' (Isaiah 2:3). On that day the law shall go out of Zion and the word of the Lord from Jerusalem. He shall then judge between the nations, and shall decide for many peoples (Isaiah 2:3–4). The Bible then forbids idolatrous practices for the Jewish nation, but is indifferent to the ways of other peoples: they are free to worship idols in the expectation that eventually they will realize the futility of such practices. Such a position is succinctly depicted by the biblical scholar Yehezkiel Kaufmann: in *The Religion of Israel:*

> This vision...may best be described as cosmic national monotheism. YHWH is the one and only God, but he has chosen Israel alone of all the nations to be his people. He governs the entire world, but he has revealed his name and his Torah only to Israel; therefore, only Israel is obliged to worship him. The

nations are judged for violations of the moral law, but never for idolatry...The Torah, thus, divides mankind into two realms: Israel, who are obliged to worship God, and the nations, who have no part in him. The idolatry of Israel is sin, but not that of the nations.

(Kaufmann, 1960, 163–4)

The Bible thus endorses a form of Jewish Exclusivism. According to Scripture the Jews are the recipients of God's true revelation and constitute his chosen people. Such a conviction led to the harsh condemnation of foreign deities and the strict admonition not to engage in idolatry. For the biblical writers, these gods are nonentities, incapable of intervening in history. None the less, foreign nations are not condemned for their idolatrous practices: idolatry is sinful only for the Jewish people, not for non-Jews. However at the end of days, according to the prophets, there will be a universal recognition that the God of Israel is the Lord of the universe, and all people will ascend to the house of the God of Jacob.

THE NOAHIDE LAWS AND IDOLATROUS PRACTICES

In the Hebrew Scriptures God is depicted as making a covenant with the Jewish nation; as his chosen people they are forbidden to worship other gods. Non-Jews on the other hand are free to engage in idolatrous practices. Thus, although Israel's covenant with God is considered superior to the religious beliefs and observances of foreign peoples, such superiority should not impel the Jewish nation to condemn those who engage in idolatry. However in the rabbinic period, such leniency underwent a major transformation. According to the rabbis, all Jews are obliged to observe the whole Torah, while every non-Jew is a 'son of the covenant of Noah'. In theory the Noahide laws are based on the commandments given to Adam and Noah; as progenitors of all human beings, the obligations placed on them are universal in scope. Traditionally these laws are: the prohibition of idolatry, blasphemy, bloodshed, sexual sins, theft, eating from a living animal, and the injunction to establish a legal system.

On this view, non-Jews are perceived as culpable if they engage in idolatrous practices, since the prohibition against idolatry is understood as prior to God's special covenant with his own people. However, a fundamental distinction is drawn between conventional idolatry as opposed to idolatry stemming from religious conviction. In this regard the Talmud records the opinion of the second century Palestinian sage Johanan:

> It is stated: R. Hanina says that one's heavenly constellation makes one wise or rich, and that Israel has its own constellation. R. Johanan said that Israel does not have its own constellation. R. Johanan said that we know Israel does not have its own constellation from the verse, 'Thus says the Lord, do not learn the way of the nations, and from the heavenly signs do not be afraid, for the nations are afraid of them' (Jeremiah 10:2) – they are afraid of them but not Israel.
>
> (Shab 156a)

In this passage Johanan appears to be repeating the previous biblical doctrine of monotheism being correct for Israel and idolatry for the gentiles. However, the key to understanding his statement concerns his choice of the Scriptural verse from Jeremiah as a proof text. Here the heavenly bodies are referred to as 'signs'; that is the nations of the world approach God through the medium of nature. Israel on the other hand must approach him directly through revealed commandments. The differences between Israel and the gentiles is not that Israel worships the one God whereas gentiles worship other gods; rather Israel worships God directly whereas the nations of the world approach him through visible intermediaries which function symbolically. On this view pagans should be understood as polytheists in practice but monotheists in theory if they worship the one God through the adoration of nature and reverence for the symbols which their culture has developed.

Given such an understanding of polytheism, gentiles are guilty of violating the Noahide ban against idolatry only if they believe in the divine nature of the objects they worship. However, if these idols are conceived as signs or symbols of the one supreme God, such behaviour is acceptable. In short gentiles are permitted to engage in polytheistic activity as long as they perceive that God is the ultimate object of their concern – in such cases they are not literally idolators.

The notion that gentile idolatry is not necessarily polytheistic in principle became a dominant motif of Hellenistic and later rabbinic

Judaism. The Jewish historian Josephus for example wrote 'Let none blaspheme the gods which other cities revere, nor rob foreign temples, nor take treasure that has been dedicated in the name of any god' (Novak, 1983, 97). Instead Josephus advocated mutual religious tolerance and respect. Such an idea is reflected in the Septuagint's translation of Exodus 22:27 'You shall not curse God' (*Elohim lo tekallel*). Here the Septuagint translates the Hebrew as *theous ou kakologeseis* ('gods you shall not curse'): the implication is that Jews should not curse the gods of other nations. Again the Hellenistic Jewish philosopher Philo prohibited Jewish ridicule of pagan cults because their ultimate intent is not essentially opposed to monotheism. Subsequently in a similar vein the Talmud interprets Malachi 1:11 ('For from the rising of the sun to its setting my name is great among the nations, and in every place incense is offered to my name, and a pure offering; for my name is great among the nations') as referring to the fact that even idolators acknowledge one supreme God.

How is this distinction between the notion of conventional idolatry and idolatry by conviction to be understood? Pure idolatry consists in the elevation of what is finite to the level of the Divine – the finite in such a case is perceived as the object of worship – it is in no way symbolic. Rather the idol is a representation of a divine being's power and wisdom: it itself is the object of devotion and veneration. Such a conception was succinctly described by the contemporary Jewish theologian, Emil Fackenheim in *Encounters between Judaism and Modern Philosophy*:

> With regard to ancient idolatry we shall fail totally if we mistake the idol for a mere religious symbol...it is not a 'symbol' at all. The ancient idol is not a finite object that distinguished itself from the Divine Infinity even as it points to it. The idol is itself divine. The idolatrous projection...is such as to produce not a symbolic but rather a literal and hence total identification of finiteness and infinitude...the ancient idol was not an irrelevance but rather the demonic rival of the One of Israel, and radically intolerable.
>
> (Fackenheim, 1973, 188–9)

Symbolism on the other hand is legitimate in pagan religions only when the objects of devotion are not elevated in this way. Monotheism demands that God alone is the ultimate object of

worship. Symbolic representation however involves the attempt
to perceive finite reality as pointing to the transcendent. In this
process objects serve simply as symbols or indicators of God's
transcendence while emphasizing their own incompleteness. In
pointing beyond themselves they direct the believer to what is
ultimate. Hence these symbols do not endeavour to displace God
– instead they function as channels to the Divine. For the rabbis
then symbolic intermediacy in gentile polytheism is acceptable as
long as the symbols themselves are not understood as having
divine status. If pagans simply follow the conventional practices
of their respective religious traditions, they are not guilty of
violating the Noahide ban on idolatry provided they believe in
One God.

Here then in rabbinic sources we can see the emergence of a new
theological conception of non-Jewish worship. In the Bible the gods
of other nations are ridiculed, and the Israelites are warned not to
turn away from worship of the God of Israel. Yet such Jewish
Exclusivism did not entail the need to persuade foreign peoples of
their misguided ways; instead the Jewish nation was simply to
remain loyal to the Covenant. Gentile idolatry was tolerated in the
expectation that in the end of days all peoples would acknowledge
the God of Israel as the Lord of history. In time however, such an
Exclusivist stance was superseded by a Jewish form of Inclusivism
which accepted pagan observance as legitimate as long as these
gentile worshippers acknowledged its symbolic function. Those
who worshipped these objects as ends in themselves were guilty of
violating the Noahide covenant; pagans who were monotheists at
heart however were free from such stigma. Rabbinic Inclusivism
was thus far more lenient about polytheistic practices than biblical
Exclusivism. Yet in one sense such Inclusivism was less tolerant:
monotheistic idolators were acceptable but not pure polytheists –
for the rabbis they were transgressing against God himself.

RABBENU TAM AND THE KABBALISTS

The rabbinic conception of Noahide Law served as the framework
for later speculation about Christianity: living in a Christian world,
Jewish sages were anxious to formulate a Jewish response to
Christian faith. As previously noted, Rabbi Johanan maintained

that gentiles are not necessarily committed to idolatry *per se* – rather many simply practise pagan rites out of ancestral custom while remaining monotheists. The central question facing Jewish scholars was whether Christians are in reality polytheists, and thus guilty of idolatry.

According to the twelfth century French scholar Rabbenu Jacob Tam, Christians are not idolators because Christianity is monotheistic in character. Rabbenu Tam's reasoning concerning this issue is illustrated by his discussion of Jewish oaths. According to the *Talmud* Jews are not permitted to enter into business partnerships with gentiles because of the probability that in their transactions gentiles would be required to take oaths in the name of foreign gods: 'The father of Samuel said that it is forbidden for a person to set up a partnership with a gentile lest the gentile become obligated to swear an oath by his god.' (Sanhedrin 63b). This ruling prohibits a Jew from being even an indirect cause for a non-Jew to swear by his god. Faced with this prescription, Rabbenu Tam interpreted the status of Christians as follows:

In this age they (Christians) all swear by their saints to whom they do not ascribe divinity. And, even though they mention God's name along with them, and their intent is for something else, nonetheless, their awareness is of the Maker of heaven and earth. Even though they associate the name of God and something else (saints) we do not find that it is forbidden indirectly to cause others to perform such association.

(Novak, 1989, 47)

Following Johanan's distinction between idolatry where the objects are themselves worshipped as opposed to where they function symbolically, Rabbenu Tam argued that Christians are permitted to acknowledge God through the mediation of saints; in such situations they are monotheistic in belief and hence do not violate Noahide law. Given this interpretation, Rabbenu Tam went on to say that Jews may enter into business association with Christians in which oaths might well be required during the course of their transactions. Here Rabbenu Tam's central point is that Christians can enter into a legitimate relationship with Jews as long as they recognize God as the Lord of all creation.

Following Rabbenu Tam's view, later medieval Jewish scholars extended this leniency to the use of trinitarian formulae in

Christian oaths. According to these thinkers, the fact that Christians believe in the Trinity does not imply that they are polytheists. Such permissiveness about trinitarian belief was conditioned by the emergence of kabbalistic theology which arose after the time of Rabbenu Tam. This mystical development within Judaism emerged as a revolt against the Aristotelian and Neoplatonic metaphysics of early medieval Jewish philosophy. In essence it rejected the philosophical assumption that any relations predicated of God are external to his divine being. For medieval philosophers the inner life of God is wholly unitary and impenetrable. Kabbalistic doctrine however asserted that there is a multiplicity within the Godhead itself.

According to the kabbalists, God in himself is beyond any speculative comprehension. To express the unknowable aspect of the Divine, kabbalistic thinkers referred to the Divine Infinite as *Ayn Sof* – the absolute perfection in which there is no distinction or plurality. The *Ayn Sof* does not reveal itself; it is beyond all thought. In kabbalistic teaching, creation is bound up with the manifestation of the hidden God and his outward movement. According to the *Zohar*, divine emanations (*sefirot*) emanate from the hidden depths of the Godhead like a flame. These *sefirot* emanate successively from above to below, each one revealing a stage in the process. The common order of the *sefirot* and the names most generally used are: (1) supreme crown; (2) wisdom; (3) intelligence; (4) greatness; (5) power; (6) beauty; (7) endurance; (8) majesty; (9) foundation; (10) kingdom.

In their totality these *sefirot* are frequently represented as a cosmic tree of emanation. It grows from its root – the first *sefirah* – and spreads downwards in the direction of the lower worlds to those *sefirot* which constitute its trunk and its main branches. Another depiction of the *sefirot* is in the form of a man: the first *sefirah* represents the head; the next three *sefirot* the cavities of the brain; the fourth and fifth *sefirot* the arms; the sixth the torso; the seventh and eighth the legs; the ninth the sexual organ; and the tenth the all-embracing totality of this image. In kabbalistic literature this heavenly man is also divided into two parts – the left column is made up of the female *sefirot* and the right column of the male. Another arrangement presents the *sefirot* as ten concentric circles, a depiction related to medieval cosmology in which the universe is understood as made up of ten spheres.

For the kabbalists the *sefirot* are dynamically structured; through them divine energy flows from its source and separates into individual channels, reuniting in the lowest *sefirah*. These *sefirot* were also understood as divine substances as well as containers of his essence; often they are portrayed as flames of fire. Yet despite their individuality, they are unified with the *Ayn Sof* in the moment of creation. According to the Zohar, all existences are emanations from the Deity – he is revealed in all things because he is immanent in them. To reconcile this process of emanation with the doctrine of creation *ex nihilo* some kabbalists argued that the *Ayn Sof* should be seen as *Ayin* (nothingness); thus the manifestation of the Divine through the *sefirot* is a self-creation out of divine nothingness.

Such speculation about plurality within the Godhead made a metaphysical rejection of Christian trinitarian claims impossible – anti-trinitarian arguments could easily be turned into a critique of kabbalistic doctrine. Thus Jewish thinkers were loath to denounce Christians as idolators despite their rejection of the doctrine of the Trinity and the Incarnation. Hence, not only veneration of the saints but also the adoration of the persons of the Trinity was regarded as acceptable. In both cases Christians appeared to view these objects simply as channels through which to approach the one Eternal God rather than as ends in and of themselves. On this view, Christians were perceived as fully within the Noahide covenant.

Here then in the view of Rabbenu Tam and later halakhists, the earlier rabbinic conception of symbolic intermediacy was applied to Christian believers. In the view of these scholars, the Jewish faith is based on an immediate relationship with God whereas Christianity involves symbolic mediation through the saints or the Persons of the Trinity: Judaism is thus the religiously superior faith. Nonetheless Christianity is not idolatry, and those who believe in Jesus are not guilty of transgressing Noahide Law. Here then Jewish Inclusivism as espoused by the rabbis embraced the Christian community as part of God's covenant with all humanity. Further, Rabbenu Tam's permissiveness about Jewish–Christian business partnerships – far removed from the Bible's harsh condemnation of the Israelites' contact with foreign peoples – provided a common moral area in which Jews and Christians could trust each other's oaths even though Christians are compelled to swear in the name of the Father, the Son and the Holy Spirit.

MOSES MAIMONIDES

In contrast with Rabbenu Tam, the twelfth century theologian Moses Maimonides drew a distinction between Islam and Christianity. In contrast with Islam, he argued that Christianity should be regarded as a form of polytheistic belief. Thus his commentary on the tractate *Avodah Zara in the Mishnah,* he stated:

> Know that this Christian nation, who advocate the messianic claim, in all their various sects, all of them are idolators. On all their festivals it is forbidden for us to deal with them. And all Torah restrictions pertaining to idolators pertain to them. Sunday is one of their festivals. Therefore, it is forbidden to deal with believers in 'the messiah' on Sunday at all in any manner whatsoever; rather, we deal with them as we would deal with any idolators on their festival.
>
> (Maimonides, 1965, vol. 2, 225)

He then went on to extend this prohibition:

> Therefore, one must know that any one of the cities of the Christian nation that has in it a place of worship, namely, a church, which is, without doubt, a house of idolatry: through that city one must not intentionally pass, let alone dwell there. But, the Lord has turned us over into the cities against our will in order to fulfil Scripture's prediction, 'you will serve their gods that are the work of human hands: wood and stone' (Deuteronomy 4:28). If this is the law pertaining to the city, all the more so does it apply to the house of idolatry itself, that it is minimally forbidden to look at it, let alone go near it, all the more so to actually enter it.
>
> (Maimonides, 1965, vol. 2, 226)

If Christians simply believed in Jesus as the Messiah, that would not render them idolators; however the fact that they use icons in worship indicates the errors of their beliefs. The judgement that Christianity is idolatrous character is reiterated in the *Mishneh Torah* where Maimonides made the following distinction:

> The resident-alien, namely one who has accepted the seven Noahide laws as we have already explained: his wine is forbidden

to drink but it is permitted to derive monetary benefit from it... Such is the case with all the gentiles who are not idolators, like these Muslims...so rule all the post-talmudic authorities. But, as for even the non-sacramental wine of those idolators, it is forbidden to derive monetary benefit from it.

(Novak, 1989, 58)

Here then Maimonides differentiated between religions which he viewed as non-idolatrous compared with idolatrous Christians. This conception is grounded in his critique of trinitarian belief. In the *Guide for the Perplexed*, Maimonides stated that Christian doctrine is polytheistic in character:

God's being One by virtue of a true Oneness, so that no composition whatever is to be found in Him and no possibility of division in any way whatever – then you must know that he, may he be exalted, has in no way and in no mode any essential attribute, and that just as it is impossible that he should be a body, it is also impossible that he should possess an essential attribute. If, however, someone believes that he is one, but possesses a certain number of essential attributes, he says in his words that he is one, but believes him in his thought to be many. This resembles what the Christians say: namely, that he is one but also three, and that three are one.

(Maimonides, 1963, 111)

According to Maimonides, Christianity is a form of polytheism since it posits plurality within the Godhead. In addition, Maimonides regarded Christianity as illegitimate since it has undermined the authority of the divine commandments and elevated Jesus above Moses. Here he implicated Islam along with the Christian faith since Islam assumes that Muhammad supersedes Moses. For Maimonides it is an error for both Christians and Muslims to assume that the authority of the Torah has been superseded by a further revelation – in making this claim these two rival faiths have distorted the divine message which was communicated to Moses on Mount Sinai.

Even though Maimonides ranked Islam higher than Christianity on theological grounds, in one sense he viewed Christianity more favourably. Asked about the talmudic ban on teaching gentiles more about the Torah than the Noahide laws he wrote:

It is permitted to teach the commandments to Christians and to draw them our religion, but this is not permitted with Muslims because of what is known to you about their belief that this Torah is not divine revelation...but the uncircumcised ones believe that the version of the Torah has not changed, only they interpret it with their faulty exegesis, it is possible that they shall return to what is best...there is nothing that they shall find in their Scriptures that differs from ours.

(Maimonides, 1960, vol. 1, 284–5)

Maimonides here insisted that since Muslims have rejected the authority of Scripture, they would not be persuaded by an appeal to the Torah – there is thus no reason to teach them about the Jewish tradition.

Despite such criticism of both Islam and Christianity, Maimonides viewed Christians and Muslims as potentially paving the way for the reign of the Messiah and the universal reign of God – this will be the full triumph of monotheism. To achieve this goal, Jews must engage in the conversion of both communities. In this enumeration of the 613 commandments in the Torah, he emphasized the duty to proclaim the truth of Judaism:

The ninth positive commandment is one which he commanded us to sanctify the divine name, which is what he said, 'and I shall be sanctified in the midst of the people of Israel' (Leviticus 22:32). The essence of the commandment which is commanded is to publicize this true faith in the world, and we should not fear any harm.

(Maimonides, 1946, 37–8)

In proclaiming the truth of their faith, Jews are to reach out to Christians and Muslims, yet the approach must be different in both cases. With Muslims, Jews are to emphasize how Judaism in doctrine and practice presents a more satisfactory form of philosophical monotheism than Islam. However, in attempting to persuade Christians of the superiority of Judaism, Jews are to stress that the Hebrew Bible reveals purer montheisitic belief than the New Testament.

In propounding this thesis, Maimonides adopted a less lenient approach to Christianity than Rabbenu Tam. Since Christians subscribe to the doctrine of the Incarnation and the Trinity, he believed they should be regarded as polytheists. Yet since they have accepted the Hebrew Scriptures as the word of God there is hope that they might be able to transcend their lapse into idolatry. What is required in achieving this end is for Jewish scholars to teach Christians the correct understanding of the Biblical text – in this way they can be brought to an acceptance of the truth of Judaism. As far as Islam is concerned, the study of Scripture will not necessarily lead Muslims to an acceptance of the superiority of Judaism. Since they do not recognize the authority of the Bible they must be exposed to the philosophical truths of Judaic monotheism. Underlying this quest to enlighten Christian and Muslims, Maimonides espoused a limited form of Jewish Inclusivism. The Islamic faith is not idolatry because Muslims are monotheists; Christianity – although idolatrous – is true in so far as Christians accept the Hebrew Scriptures as revelation. None the less Muslims and Christians are in need of instruction so that they will recognize the errors of their ways and accept Judaism as the true faith.

JUDAH HALEVI

Unlike Maimonides the eleventh-century Spanish theologian Judah Halevi adopted a more positive approach to Christianity and Islam. In his theological dialogue, the *Kuzari*, he depicted a pagan king who attempted to discover the true religion. After being told in a dream that although his intentions were acceptable to God his actions were not, he invited an Aristotelian philosopher, and representatives of Islam, Christianity and Judaism to discuss the respective merits of their traditions. This literary framework provides a setting for a comparison between the three monotheistic faiths. In the beginning of the work the philosopher, the Christian and the philosopher expounded their opinions. When the king saw that both Christianity and Islam are based on Judaism he called in the Jewish scholar.

At the outset the king explained that he had not originally intended to question the Jew 'because I am aware of the destruction of their books and of their narrow minded views, their misfortunes having deprived them of all commendable qualities' (Halevi, 1965, 33). Yet, because Christianity and Islam are derived from Judaism, he was anxious to hear the rabbi's opinions. As an opening statement the rabbi declared:

I believe in the God of Abraham, Isaac and Israel, who led the Israelites out of Egypt with signs and miracles; who fed them in the desert and gave them the land, after having made them traverse the sea and the Jordan in a miraculous way; who sent Moses with this Law, and subsequently thousands of prophets who confirmed his Law by promises to those who observed, and threats to the disobedient. We believe in what is contained in the Torah – a very large domain.

(Halevi, 1965, 33)

After expressing his views about various philosophical theories concerning eternity and nature, the rabbi discussed the origin of the Jewish faith. The Israelites, he stressed, lived in Egypt as slaves, but looked forward to the promise given to their ancestors – Abraham, Isaac and Jacob, that they would inherit the land of Palestine. After Moses led the children of Israel out of bondage, they wandered in the desert for 40 years. During this period God revealed the Torah to Moses on Mount Sinai. In recounting these events, the rabbi emphasized the pre-eminence of the Jewish people:

Bear with me a little and I will prove the pre-eminence of the people. For me it is sufficient that God chose them as his community and people from all the nations of the world; that the Divine power descended on the whole people, so that they all became worthy to be addressed by him...up to that time the power had descended from Adam on isolated individuals only.

(Halevi, 1965, 45)

After this confrontation the king and his vizier travelled to deserted mountains on the seashore; they arrived at night when some Jews were celebrating the Sabbath. They disclosed their identity, embraced their religion, were circumcised in the cave, and returned to their country. The king studied the Torah as well as the books of the prophets, and employed the rabbi as his teacher. In their discussions, the king put many questions to him concerning Hebrew expressions. The first referred to the names and attributes ascribed to God: their seeming anthropomorphism was puzzling since it was apparently opposed to reason. Such terms, the rabbi explained must be understood metaphorically.

The king then questioned the rabbi about the pre-eminence of the land of Israel. Were the prophets not in other places? he inquired. In response the rabbi declared:

The land was appointed for the instruction of mankind and apportioned to the tribes of Israel from time to the confusion of tongues, as it is said: 'When the Most High divided among the nations of their inheritance, when separated the sons of Man, he set up the frontiers of the nations according to the number of the sons of Israel.'

(Deuteronomy 32:8) (Halevi, 1965, 67–8)

The rabbi then discoursed on the nature of Jewish religious duties; here he described the life of a pious person. In contrast with the Greek philosophical ideal, the Jewish ideal prototype is based on a religious foundation that embraces all of life as a divine creation. In the fulfilment of his religious obligations, such an individual is able to experience a degree of joy not open to other religions. In this context the rabbi pointed out that the Sabbath cannot mean for the Muslim or Christian what it signifies for the Jew who is reminded in its celebration of the Exodus from Egypt. The rabbi then went on to defend the rabbinic tradition against Karaites who have rejected the chain of rabbinic interpretation as well as Christians who have set aside the authority of the Torah.

In the following section of the *Kuzari* the rabbi examined the names of God; during the course of this investigation he pointed out that prophecy is the result of being in the presence of the *Shekinah*. In addition, he focussed on the uniqueness of the nation which alone possesses the faculty of prophecy. In the final part of the *Kuzari* the rabbi resolved to leave the land of the Khazars for Jerusalem. Regretting this parting, the king asked what can be sought in Palestine since the *Shekinah* is absent from it. 'Why dost thou expose thyself to the dangers of land and sea and to risks incurred by contact with other people? (Halevi, 1965, 126). In response the rabbi stated that although the visible *Shekinah* has disappeared, 'the invisible and spiritual *Shekinah* is with every born Israelite of pure life, pure heart and sincere devotion to the Lord of Israel. And Palestine has a special relation to the Lord of Israel. Pure life can be perfect only there' (Halevi, 1965, 126).

In this apology for Judaism, Halevi expressed his conviction of the absolute superiority of Judaism. As a result of the rabbi's defence, the king of the Khazars chose the Jewish religion over both Islam and Christianity largely because these two faiths are derived from it – Judaism, the king believed, is the original and most pure source of monotheism. In arguing that Judaism is the only mono-theistic faith that has not been adulterated by outside influences,

Halevi reversed the successionist claims of both Islam and Christianity: instead of embodying a true fulfilment of God's revelation, they have diluted the original revelation from God. Yet despite Halevi's conviction that Judaism is the supremely true faith, he believed that these two rival religions have the potentiality to spread the message of monotheism: Christians as well as Muslims can play a preparatory role in the unfolding of God's plan for all humanity– because they are in a state of monotheistic potentiality, they possess a messianic preparatory function. In the *Kuzari* then while defending Judaism Halevi espoused a type of Jewish Inclusivism akin to that propounded by Rabbenu Tam. Unlike Maimonides, he viewed Christians as monotheists: for this reason, they along with the Muslim community can prepare the world for the final redemption in which all humankind will recognize that the God of Israel is the Lord of all creation.

3

Medieval Conflict between Jews and Christians

Even though such writers as Rabbenu Tam and Judah Halevi espoused a tolerant attitude toward the Christian faith, the Jewish community as a whole was antagonistic to Christianity throughout the Middle Ages. This was not surprising considering that throughout Europe Jews were continually attacked and accused of such crimes as murdering Christian children and using their blood for ritual purposes, defaming the host, blaspheming Christ, and bringing about the Black Plague. Such hostility toward Judaism was intensified by a series of disputations between Christians and Jews in the thirteenth and early fifteenth centuries. The first of these confrontations took place in Paris in 1240: the purpose of this encounter was to assertain whether the Talmud contains blasphemies against Jesus and the Christian faith. Despite a spirited defense by the Jewish participants, this interrogation resulted in the condemnation and burning of the Talmud. Two decades later a second disputation occurred in Spain presided over by the King of Aragon: the purpose of this confrontation was to convert the Jewish populace. In his response to the Christian delegates the Jewish scholar Nahmanides was permitted to defend the Jewish tradition, yet again such a confrontation caused considerable alarm among Jewry. The third disputation occurred in Tortosa from 1413–14. Unlike the previous two encounters, this event lasted for nearly two years and was presided over by Pope Benedict XIII. Throughout these months the Jewish community was terrified of the outcome, and feared for their safety. Thus during these centuries of turmoil and instability Jews lived in the shadow of a crusading and triumphant Church; as a result there was little attempt (with the previous notable exceptions) to formulate a positive assessment of Christianity or of any other faith.

CHRISTIAN MASSACRE AND MURDER

Despite the existence of isolated positive Jewish responses to
Christianity in the Middle Ages, the Christian onslaught on Jewry
during this period prevented the development of a more general
acceptance of Christianity. Shortly after the year 1000, rumours
began to circulate in Christian lands about the 'Prince of Babylon'
who had brought about the destruction of Christians at the instiga-
tion of the Jews. In response, princes, bishops and townsfolk sought
revenge against the Jewish population, and attacks took place in
Rouen, Orleans, Limoges, Mainz, and elsewhere. Jews were
converted by force or killed. At the end of the eleventh century,
Pope Urban II preached the First Crusade at the Council of
Clermont-Ferrand. As Christian knights, monks and commoners
set out on their holy mission, they took revenge on Jewish infidels
living in Christian lands.

In the Rhine valley, where Jewish communities were probably the
most numerous in Europe, the most horrendous massacres
occurred. As bands led by French and German lords swept through
the Rhineland, Jews were mercilessly slaughtered. Although
bishops and noblemen protected the Jews in various cities where
they were under threat, Jewish communities throughout Europe
were besieged and thousands of Jews lost their lives in this onslaught. Yet despite these massacres European Jewry was able to
resume their former existence in the following decades. However in
1146 Pope Eugenius III and St Bernard of Clairvaux preached a new
Crusade which was accompanied by anti-Jewish sentiment. Later in
the twelfth century the Third Crusade led to massacres in London,
York, Norwich and Stamford and Lynn. These crusades and their
aftermath brought into focus Christian contempt for the Jews who
stubbornly clung to their ancestral faith. These were the villainous
figures of the New Testament, the people castigated by the Church
Fathers. Unlike Jewish thinkers who believed that all those who
subscribe to the Noahide Laws can be saved, Christian apologists
argued that the only salvation for Jewry was to turn from their
foolish ways and embrace true faith. During these centuries Jews
were also accused of committing murder for magical purposes.
Throughout Europe Jews were charged with murdering Christian
children to incorporate their blood in the preparation of unleavened
bread for the Passover. The first case of such a ritual murder took
place in 1144 in Norwich England. The body of a young apprentice

was discovered on the evening of Good Friday in a wood; it was
rumoured that he had been killed by Jews. According to tradition,
this murder had been planned by a meeting of rabbis which took
place at Narbonne. Although the Church authorities attempted to
protect the Jewish population, riots took place and a leading Jewish
figure was killed by a knight who was his debtor. The next case
occurred in Wurzburg in 1147 during the Second Crusade when the
body of a Christian was found and Jews of the city were blamed for
his death.

Three years later a different allegation appeared: the Jews were
censured for profaning the Host. Thus Jean d'Outremeuse, the
chronicler of Liège, alleged that:

> In this year, it happened at Cologne that the son of a converted
> Jew went on Easter day to church, in order to receive the body of
> God, along with others he took it into his mouth and quickly bore
> it to his house; but when he returned from the Church, he grew
> afraid and in his distress made a hole in the ground and buried
> the Host within it; but a priest came along, opened the hole, and
> in it found the shape of a child, which he intended to bear to the
> church but there came from the sky a great light, the child was
> raised out of the priest's hands and borne up to heaven.
>
> (Poliakov, 1965, vol. 1, 59)

Although accusations of ritual murder were infrequent at first,
several cases took place in England at the end of the twelfth
century, and subsequently they spread to the continent. Despite
church pronouncements clearing the Jews of such horrendous
charges, accusations of ritual murder and the profonanation of the
Host continued to circulate. In consequence Jewry was subjected to
continual persecution. Jews during this period were thus victimized for atrocious acts even though church authorities decreed that
these charges were groundless. By libelling the Jews in this manner,
the Jewish community was portrayed as sadistic, thirsting for
Christian blood – not surprisingly such allegations inflamed the
hatred of Jewry for the Christian masses.

Such Jewish–Christian hostility was further exacerbated by a
series of decrees promulgated by the Fourth Lateran Council in
1215. Nearly 1500 churchmen from throughout the Christian world
endorsed the decisions taken by Pope Innocent III. Regarding
Jewish clothing, the Council stated:

In the countries where Christians do not distinguish themselves from Jews it is decreed that henceforth Jews of both sexes will be distinguished from other peoples by their garments, as moreover has been described unto them by Moses. They will not show themselves in public during Holy Week, for some of them on these days wear their finest garments and mock the Christians clad in mourning. Trespassers will be duly punished by the secular powers, in order that they no longer dare flout Christ in the presence of Christians.

(Poliakov, 1965, vol. 1, 64)

The enforcement of such provisions differed from country to country. In France a circular badge of yellow cloth was worn. From the thirteenth to the fourteenth centuries, twelve Councils and nine Royal decrees insisted on the strict observance of this law. In 1361, when King John the Good recalled the Jews to France after their exile, he ordered them to wear an insignia which was half red and half white. In Germany a particular type of hat was worn rather than a badge of clothing; texts from fourteenth and fifteenth centuries refer to this hat as red and yellow, but in the following centuries a badge took its place. In Poland Jews were required to wear a pointed green hat, whereas in England strips of cloth were sewn across the chest often in the shape of Tablets of Law. In Spain and Italy an insignia was worn. These various distinguishing marks impressed on the minds of gentiles the differences between Christians and Jews, encouraging Jews to detest the Christian community which had stigmatised them in this way.

During this period the newly instituted Inquisition under the control of the Dominicans was charged with the responsibility of eliminating all heretical views. The Dominicans were anxious to uproot all heresies, and they took an active interest in Jewish doctrine. At the beginning of the thirteenth century these protectors of Church orthodoxy were disturbed that Aristotelian concepts had penetrated into European thought through Arabic and Jewish translations. In 1210 and 1215 the Church condemned Aristotle's *Physics* and *Metaphysics*, and in 1228 Pope Gregory IX forbade contact with Greek philosophy. Such antipathy to philosophical speculation provoked two rabbis to unite forces with the Dominicans of Montpellier. Addressing the Church authorities, they asked: 'Why do you pay no attention to our heretics and our atheists corrupted by the doctrine of Moses of Egypt (Moses

Maimonides), author of impious works? Since you are uprooting your heresies, uproot ours as well, and order the burning of the wicked books.' (Poliakov, 1965, vol. 1, 68–9).

As a result of such entreaties, the Inquisition took an interest in Jewish sources, particularly the Talmud. An apostate of Judaism, Nicholas Donin (who had become a Dominican brother of la Rochelle) travelled to Rome to inform Pope Gregory IX that the Talmud contains blasphemies against the Christian faith. As a consequence the Pope urged the kings of France, England, Castile and Aragon to investigate this claim. In France Louis IX initiated such an investigation and copies of the Talmud were confiscated. In 1240 a public debate was held in Paris between Jewish and Christian scholars. The hostility engendered by such claims is reflected in minnesingers of the period such as Konrad von Wurzburg:

> Woe to the cowardly Jews, deaf and wicked,
> Who have no care to save themselves from the sufferings
> of hell.
> The Talmud has corrupted them and made them lose
> their honour.
> It would be well to forbid their heretical Talmud,
> A false and ignoble book.
> (Poliakov, 1965, vol. 1, 71)

Given such a climate of anti-Jewish sentiment, there was little enthusiasm among Jews during this period to formulate a positive assessment of the Christian faith.

THE PARIS DISPUTATION OF 1240

In the Paris Disputation which took place in 1240, Christian adversaries argued that the Talmud should be destroyed since it serves as a rival to Scripture and also contains attacks on the Christian faith. The Christian side was led by Nicholas Donin, a converted Jew who was opposed to the rabbinic tradition; on the Jewish side Rabbi Yehiel ben Joseph of Paris, a prominent Talmudist, was joined by three other rabbis. The disputation itself was initiated by a letter sent by Pope Gregory IX to the Kings of Christendom complaining about the Talmud.

According to the Jewish account of this disputation, Donin argued that the Talmud contains various blasphemies against Jesus: For example, the Talmud says that Jesus is in hell, and his punishment is to be immersed in boiling excrement (Gitt. 56b). In response Yehiel declared.

> This Jesus mentioned here by the Talmud, is another Jesus, not the one whom Christians worship. This was a certain Jesus who mocked the words of the sages, and believed only in the written Scripture like you. You can tell this, because he is not called 'Jesus of Nazareth', but simply 'Jesus'.
>
> (Maccoby, 1982, 156)

Undeterred, Donin quoted another passage (Sanh. 43a) which uses the expression 'Jesus of Nazareth': 'When Jesus went forth to be stoned, a herald went out before him for forty days, crying, "Jesus the Nazarene goes forth to be stoned because he practised sorcery and enticed to idolatry, and perverted others of Israel. Anyone who knows anything in his favour, let him come and speak in his favour."' Donin then continued: 'Here is another passage in which both Jesus and Mary are blasphemed (Sanh. 67a). The passage says that someone called Ben Stada, otherwise known as Ben Pandira, was hanged in Lydda on the eve of Passover. His mother's name was Miriam, "the hairdresser"; her husband's name was Pappos ben Judah, and her lover's name was Pandira. So Mary is called an adulteress by the Talmud.' (Maccoby, 1982, 157)

In reply Yehiel stated that 'Mary was our flesh and bone, and we have nothing to say against her, for the Talmud does not even mention her. The "Miriam" mentioned in the passage quoted by Donin cannot be the same person as Mary, for the locality mentioned is Lydda, not Jerusalem, where Jesus' death took place, and where his Sepulchre is still to be seen. Moreover, Jesus is not even mentioned by name in this passage.' (Maccoby, 1982, 157)

Not put off, Donin continued:

> There is another blasphemous passage in the Talmud about Jesus. This tells (San. 107) that Jesus was a pupil of Rabbi Joshua ben Perachia, who fled to Alexandria, accompanied by Jesus to escape the persecution of King Janna. Later, on his return from Alexandria, he stayed with Jesus at an inn. Here Jesus offended his teacher by paying too much attention to the inn-keeper's

wife. Jesus wished to be forgiven, but Rabbi Joshua was too slow to forgive him, and Jesus in despair went away and put up a brick and worshipped it.

(Maccoby, 1982, 157)

Again Rabbi Yehiel asserted that this Jesus cannot be the same Jesus whom Christians worship.

Turning to other charges, Donin claimed that the Talmud permits Jews to spill the blood of gentiles. Thus Sof.15 states 'the best gentile may be killed'. In defence Rabbi Yehiel stated that an important phrase is here missing: 'the best gentile may be killed in time of war.' 'Has not God warned us and all other nations not to shed blood, by saying in his Ten Commandments, 'Thou shalt not kill'. (Maccoby, 1982, 159). Donin then asked whether Christians can be saved according to the Jewish faith. Following rabbinic tradition, Rabbi Yehiel stated: 'You may be saved if you keep the Seven Laws of the Sons of Noah, which were given to all mankind.' (Maccoby, 1982, 159).

Rabbi Yehiel then went on to explain that in the Eighteen Benedictions, the prayer which calls for punishment on the kingdoms of wickedness does not refer to the Christians. Rather 'the kingdoms of wickedness' refers to the kingdoms who in the past persecuted the Jewish people such as Egypt, Assyria and Babylon. These empires massacred and exiled Israel, and thus deserve this designation. But, he continued, 'as for this kingdom and the Pope who has given strict orders for our protection and preservation, it is incredible that we should return evil for good. And even if some individuals have harmed us, that does not mean that we are angry at the whole nation. It would not occur to us to do this; on the contrary, it was about such a nation as this that the Talmud has instructed us, "Pray for the peace of the kingdom".' (Maccoby, 1982, 160).

Donin then turned to passages in the Talmud which discriminate against gentiles:

The Talmud contains many passages directed against gentiles, saying (a) a gentile may be left to die, though not actually killed; (b) a Jew who kills a gentile is not liable to the death penalty, whereas a gentile who kills a Jew is liable; (c) it is permitted to steal the money of a gentile; (d) a Jew must not drink wine touched by a gentile; (e) one may mock gentile religion; (f) gentiles are presumed to be habituated to adultery, bestiality and homosexuality; (g) it is forbidden to help a gentile woman to give birth or to suckle her child; (h) it is forbidden to praise the beauty of a gentile.

Again, Yehiel argued that the 'gentiles' referred to here are not Christians. As proof of this, he explained, it is obvious that Jews engage in business transactions with Christians. According to the Talmud such activity is forbidden with 'gentiles'. Further Jews have much social intercourse with Christians; again, such activity is forbidden by the Talmud with 'gentiles'. The term 'gentiles' is thus meant to refer to ancient Egyptians and Canaanites who were steeped in immorality of every kind. Finally, Yehiel pointed out that Jews teach Hebrew to Christians – an activity forbidden to 'gentiles'. Replying to such claims, Donin stated that the Eighteen Benedictions contains a prayer for the destruction of heretics and slanders – this, he maintained, refers to Christians as was affirmed by the medieval commentator Rashi. In reply Yehiel argued that this passage refers to apostates from Judaism and to Karaites rather than Christians. As for Rashi's explanation, this is not authoritative.

This dialogue between Donin and Yehiel was not in fact a real disputation but rather an interrogation in which Yehiel was given little scope to explain Jewish teaching about the status of non-Jews: The Paris Disputation of 1240 was a trial of the Talmud in which Yehiel served as a witness for the defense. In the course of this inquisition, Yehiel attempted to illustrate that the Talmud does not seek to defame either Jesus or Christian belief; instead, he insisted, the derogatory statements about 'gentile' nations do not refer to the Christian community but to earlier peoples who persecuted the Jews. Further, Yehiel emphasized that Christians can be saved if they observe the Noahide Covenant. Yet, despite Yehiel's defence, the Disputation of 1240 contributed to the deterioration of Jewish-Christian understanding, and in the years that followed, the Talmud was condemned and burned and both Jews and Christians continued to regard one another with suspicion and hostility.

THE BARCELONA DISPUTATION OF 1263

The Barcelona Disputation was the most important disputation between Christians and Jews in the Middle Ages. Presided over by

King James of Aragon, the debate encouraged freedom of expression: although the Jewish participants were not at liberty to put questions against Christianity they were allowed to express opinions about the concept of the Messiah, original sin, and biblical and rabbinic exegesis. Thus unlike the Disputation at Paris where the Talmud was put on trial, this encounter between the two faiths encouraged a genuine exchange of views despite the Church's intention to convert the Jewish population.

At the beginning of the Disputation, the Jewish scholar Nahmanides stated that he wished only to discuss those matters which are fundamental to the Jewish and Christian traditions. In reply the Christian interlocutors expressed their approval of this approach. As Nahmanides wrote:

> We agreed to speak on whether the Messiah was truly divine, or entirely human, born from a man and a woman. And after that he would discuss whether the Jews still possess the true law, or whether the Christians practise it.
>
> (Maccoby, 1982, 103)

Following this plan, those representing the Christian side, principally the Jewish apostate Pablo Christiani, attempted to prove that Jesus is the Messiah on the basis of aggadic sources. In response Nahmanides strove to illustrate that such texts have been incorrectly interpretated. Countering the claim that Jesus is the Messiah, Nahmanides pointed out that Jesus never had any power; rather during his lifetime he could not even save himself. Even after his death, he did not exercise any rule. Further, Nahmanides stressed that the prophetic predictions in Scripture have not been fulfilled:

> The prophet says that in the time of the Messiah, 'And no longer shall each man teach his neighbour and each his brother, saying, "Know the Lord", for they shall all know me.' (Jeremiah 31:34); also, 'The earth shall be full of the knowledge of the Lord as the waters cover the sea' (Isaiah 11:9); also, 'They shall beat their swords into ploughshares... nation shall not lift up sword against nation, neither shall learn war any more (Isaiah 2:4). Yet from the days of Jesus until now, the whole world has been full of violence and plundering.'
>
> (Maccoby, 1982, 121)

In addition, Nahmanides emphasized that Jesus did not fulfil the messianic task of bringing about the ingathering of the exiles, rebuilding the Temple, or ruling in majesty:

> But your Messiah, Jesus did not gather one man of them, and did not even live in the time of the Exile. It is also the task of the Messiah to build the Temple in Jerusalem, but Jesus did not carry out anything in connection with the Temple, either building or destruction. Also the Messiah will rule over the peoples, and Jesus did not rule even over himself.
>
> (Maccoby, 1982, 132)

Turning to the question whether Jesus is God Incarnate, Nahmanides argued that such a belief is irrational. 'The doctrine in which you believe,' he stated, 'and which is the foundation of your faith cannot be accepted by reason, and nature affords no ground for it, nor have the prophets ever expressed it. Nor can even the miraculous stretch as far as this.' (Maccoby, 1982, p.120). In Judaism, he went on, the Messiah is conceived as completely human, of the stock of David as Scripture records: 'And there shall come forth a rod out of the stem of Jesse' (Isaiah 11:1). If Jesus were in fact born by the Spirit of God, he would not fulfil this prophecy. Even if he lodged in the womb of a woman who was of the seed of Jesse, he would not inherit the kingdom of David because neither daughters nor their progeny have this right. In reply the King cited Psalm 110:1: 'A Psalm of David; the Lord said to my Lord: Sit thou at my right hand.' Referring to this verse the Jewish apostate Pablo Christiani asked who 'King David calls my Lord' other than a divine personage. How, he asked, could a human being sit at the right hand of God? In reply Nahmanides maintained that King David composed the Psalms so that they should be sung by the Levites before the altar of the Lord. Consequently he was forced to composed the psalm in a style which was suitable for a Levite to sing. If he had written, 'The Lord said to me'; the Levite would have been saying falsehood; but it was quite fitting for the Levite to say in the sanctuary, 'The Lord said to me' The Lord said to my Lord' (i.e. David). 'Sit at my right hand'; the meaning of this 'sitting' is that the Holy One, blessed be he, would guard him all my life...And this is what meant by 'the right hand' of God. (Maccoby, 1982, 135–6).

Continuing this dialogue Pablo Christian cited *Bereshit Rabbah* 2:14: 'And the Spirit of God hovered over the face of the waters' (Genesis 1:2) – this is the spirit of the Messiah. If so, the Messiah is not a man, but the Spirit of God'. (Maccoby, 1982, p. 140). Rebuking his interlocutor, Nahmanides replied:

> Woe to him who knows nothing, and thinks that he is wise and learned. It is also said there (8:1), 'And the spirit of God hovered – this is spirit of Adam, does this reply mean that Adam would be a divine being? But someone who does not know 'what is above or what is below' in books, turns upside down the words of the living God'.
>
> (Maccoby, 1982, 140)

On the Sabbath following the disputation, the King and the Preaching Friars visited the synagogue. There the Christian scholar Raymond of Peñaforte preached about the Trinity. When he finished, Nahmanides delivered a speech criticising the doctrine:

> Harken and listen to my voice, Jews and Gentiles. 'Fra Paul (Pablo Christiani) asked me in Gerone whether I believed in the Trinity. I said, 'What is the Trinity? Does it mean that the Deity has three physical bodies such as those of human beings?' Said he, 'No'. Does it mean, then, that the Deity has three refined entities, such as souls or angelic beings?' Said he, 'No'. Does it mean one entity derived from three, as bodies are derived from the four elements?' Said he, 'No', 'If so, what is the Trinity?' Said he, 'Wisdom, will and power'. So I said, I agree that God is wise, and not foolish, that he wills, and is not inert, that he is powerful, and not powerless; but the expression 'Trinity' is a complete mistake.
>
> (Maccoby, 1982, 144–45)

When he finished Pablo Christiani stood up and affirmed that he believed in a perfect Unity, and together with it the Trinity, and that this is a matter so deep that even the angels and princes on high do not understand it. In response Nahmanides disagreed: 'It is obvious', he proclaimed, 'that a person cannot believe what he does not know; which means that the angels do not believe in the Trinity', (Maccoby, 1982, 146).

This disputation occurred at the end of the Golden Age of Spain and reflects the generally tolerant attitude of the period. Although Nahmanides was initially reluctant to take part, there was no threat of the burning of the Talmud as a result. The Church's objective was not to find Jewry guilty of blasphemy, but to draw the Jewish community to the Christian faith. In this respect the tone of the arguments used by Christian participants was more conciliatory that in Paris. Moreover the fact that Christians cited rabbinic sources indicates a degree of respect for the Jewish heritage. None the less, such a confrontation evoked considerable alarm among Spanish Jewry, inducing a fear of the Church which they regarded as meddlesome and dangerous.

THE BLACK PLAGUE AND THE JEWISH REACTION

From 1347 to 1350 the Black Plague destroyed one-third of Europe's population. According to Boccaccio's account:

> In the cities, men fell sick by thousands, and lacking care and aid, almost all died. In the morning their bodies were found at the doors of the houses where no further account was taken of a dying man than is today taken of the merest cattle. Nor were the villages spared. Lacking the succour of a physician, without the aid of any servant, the poor and wretched farmers perished with their families by day, by night, on their farms, and in their isolated houses, on the roads, and even in the fields. Then they abandoned their customs, even as the city dwellers: they no longer took any concern for their affairs nor for themselves; all, expecting to die from one day to the next, thought neither of working not of putting by the fruits of their past labours, but sought rather to consume what they had before them.
>
> (Poliakov, 1965, vol. 1, 107–8)

This catastrophe was the last in the chain of events affecting the Jewish community. According to medieval scholars, the plague was due to an unfavourable conjunction of the planets as well as the pollution of the air and poisoning of the waters. For ordinary persons, however, it was seen as a divine punishment, or the act of Satan who was in league with the Jews. In Savoy, Jacob Pascal of Toledo was accused of distributing deadly drugs to co-religionists in Cambery. As a result of this charge, Jews were arrested in Thonon, Chillon and Le Chatelard, and confessed under torture. From Savoy the legend spread to Switzerland, where various executions took place. Despite this intervention, Germans continued to massacre Jews in Colmar, Worms, Oppenheim, Frankfurt, Erfurt, Cologne and Hanover. Jews were also attacked for religious reasons. Bands of flagellants wandered throughout Germany and France, mortifying themselves in order to avert God's wrath. Such exhibitions frequently culminated in the massacre of the Jewish population. As the chronicler Jean d'Outremeuse explained:

> The good cities were full of these Flagellants and the street as well...they began to forget the service and ritual of the Holy Church, and maintained in their folly and their presumption that their rites and their songs were finer and more worthy than the ceremonies of the priests and clerics...In the time when these Flagellants went, among the countries...it was commonly said and certainly believed that this epidemic came from the Jews, and that the Jews had cast great poisons in the wells and springs throughout the world, in order to sow the plague and poison Christendom; which was why great and small alike had great choler against the Jews, who were everywhere taken where they could be held, and put to death and burned in all the regions where the Flagellants came and went.
>
> (Poliakov, 1965, vol. 1, 112)

In Germany it was widely believed that the Jews were immune to the plague. None the less, some chroniclers maintained that such an explanation was unlikely. Thus the chronicler Conrad von Meganberg reported:

> In many wells, bags filled with poison were found, and a countless number of Jews were massacred in the Rhineland, in Franconia, and in all the German countries. In truth, I do not know whether certain Jews had done this. Had it been thus, assuredly the evil would have been worse. But I know, on the other hand, that no German city had so many Jews as Vienna, and so many of them there succumbed to the plague that they were obliged to enlarge their cemetery greatly and to buy more buildings. They would have been very stupid to poison themselves.
>
> (Poliakov, 1965, vol. 1, 113)

Throughout Germany most major Jewish communities were destroyed by the plague; indeed the German population was so decimated by this disaster that in subsequent years a number of cities such as Speyer invited Jews to live in their midst with promises of protection and security. Slowly Jewish communities were reconstituted and Jewish life began anew.

The massacres of this period and those of previous centuries traumatized Jewish communities. Some of their reactions were incorporated into the Jewish liturgy; others served as the basis of religious chants. In various chronicles of these centuries Jewish animosity towards Christianity was expressed in the most vehement terms. Solomon bar Simon for example declared:

> The pope of sinful Rome rose up and urged all the peoples of Edom to believe in the Christ crucified: to unite in order to Jerusalem and conquer the city so that the strayed might returned to the site of their shame, to the tomb of him whom they have chosen as their God...Let the bones of Emico, the persecutor of the Jews be ground in a mill of fire!...O God of vengeance, O Lord God of vengeance, appear! It is for thee that we have let ourselves be slaughtered every day. Return sevenfold the wrongs of neighbours so that they may curse you! Before our very eyes let the nations be punished for the blood of thy servants that they have shed.'
>
> (Poliakov, 1965, vol. 1, 84)

In addition, numerous literary works of this period exhorted God to meet out divine justice on the Christian community. Thus in a poem about the martyrdom of Isaac (chatelain of Troyes) and his family who were tried for ritual murder, the author appealed to God for justice:

> Sinners have come for Isaac Cohen,
> He must abjure, or perish.
> He says: 'What do you want of me? For God I will die.
> As priest, I will offer him the sacrifice of my body.'
> 'You cannot escape, we hold you fast
> Become a Christian', but he swiftly replies: 'No.
> For the dogs, I would not leave God nor his name!'
> Than Haim was called, the master of Brinon,
> And another kadosh was led forth;
> Then they thrust him into a slow fire
> And with good heart he prayed to God often and low,
> Gently suffering his pain in the name of the living God.

God of vengeance, jealous God, avenger on our foes!
From awaiting your vengeance, the day seems long to us.

(Poliakov, 1965, vol. 1, 85–6)

Those who perished in the Christian onslaught and remained
faithful to their ancestral faith were regarded as hallowing God's
name. In their heroism and faithfulness, these victims cried out to
God for revenge. Hatred and faithfulness were thus mixed together
in the blood and tears of those who perished in these terrible
centuries of suffering.

THE TORTOSA DISPUTATION OF 1413–14

The most splendid disputation of the Middle Ages was held in
Tortosa; instead of lasting only several days, this event took place
for twenty-one months. In contrast with the Barcelona Disputation,
this debate was presided over by Pope Benedict XIII who summoned Jewish representatives from Aragon and Catalonia; the
purpose of this disputation was to convert the entire Jewish
populace. In this confrontation the main Christian spokesman was
the Jewish convert Geronimo de Santa Fé (Joshua Halorki), a more
learned scholar than the leading Christian participant of the
Barcelona Disputation, Pablo Christiani. On the Jewish side, the
representatives frequently referred to the arguments previously
used by Nahmanides in Barcelona.

Like the Paris Disputation, the conditions under which this
debate took place were ominous for the Jewish community. At the
end of the previous century Spanish Jewry had been massacred in
an onslaught inspired by religious enthusiasts that originated in
Castile and spread to Aragon and Catalonia – because the Jewish
population ceased to be necessary to the king and aristocracy, the
authorities were slow to respond. In the aftermath, many Jews were
forced into baptism and faced death at the hands of the Inquisition
if they endeavoured to return to Judaism. These calamitous circumstances were made even more perilous by the preaching of Vincent
Ferrer, a Dominican priest, who together with bands of flagellants
stirred up anti-Jewish animosity.

It was in this atmosphere of religious frenzy that rabbis took part
in the disputation. According to Astruk Halevi (one of the leading

Jewish figures in the discussion) this confrontation caused considerable hardship:

> We are away from our homes; our resources have diminished and are almost entirely destroyed; huge damage is resulting in our communities from our wives and children; we have inadequate maintenance here and even lack of food and are put to extraordinary expenses. Why should people suffering such woes be held accountable for their arguments?
>
> (Maccoby, 1982, 84)

The Hebrew account of this event begins with an explanation of the origin of this disputation:

> A shoot that went forth from us and thought to destroy us, and bring low down to the earth our religion of truth – is it not Joshua Halorki? He made plans to pervert us, to show that he was a true Christian and faithful to his new religion, and he asked the Pope to command the leading Jewish scholars to come before him for he wished to prove from their own Talmud that the Messiah had come; and he said to the Pope that when he proved this, it would be fitting to force them to adopt the Christian religion, when he showed true proofs before his high Holiness.
>
> (Maccoby, 1982, 168)

After the Jewish representatives appeared before the Pope, he delivered a speech in which he attempted to reassure them that they had nothing to fear from this encounter:

> Worthies of the people of the Jews, who were chosen by Him who chose them in days of old, even though they were rejected for their sins! Do not be afraid of the Disputation, for you will not receive any oppression or mal-treatment in my presence. Let your thoughts be at rest, and speak with a firm heart. Do not fear and do not tremble. Maestre Geronimo said that he wished to prove that the Messiah had come, and this from your own Talmud. It will be seen in our presence whether the truth is in his mouth or he has dreamed a dream; but as for you, do not be afraid of him, for in matters of disputation there is equality. And now go and rest in your lodgings and tomorrow morning come to me.
>
> (Maccoby, 1982, 170)

When the Jewish representatives reassembled the next day, they were confronted by a formidable Christian gathering of over one thousand including seventy prelates (cardinals, bishops and archbishops). At the outset the Pope stated that the had not sent for the Jews to decide which of the two religions is true, for as he emphasised 'it is a known thing with me that my religion and faith is true, and that your Torah was once true but was abolished'. (Maccoby, 1982, 170). Rather the purpose of the debate was to demonstrate from the Talmud and rabbinic literature that the Messiah had come. Deeply troubled by this investigation, the Jewish populace implored the Pope to free them from the disputation; when he refused they 'went to the synagogue, where there was a great gathering, and with a voice of weeping and entreaty we prayed to the Rock or our salvation that he should turn our darkness into light, and that there should not go forth from our mouths a stumbling-block, before all those lions who stood against us'. (Maccoby, 1982, 171)

Resolutely the Jewish representatives defended their faith. In face of Geronimo de Santa Fe's criticisms, the delegates affirmed that it was not out of obstinacy that Jews have remained loyal to the tradition of their ancestors; rather the nation upheld the Torah because it was given in the presence of 600 000 with strong signs and God's revelation. R. Matithiah then stated that the Jewish tradition curses those who attempt to demonstrate when the Messiah will come. God, he declared, has hidden this from all the peoples and from all the prophets. At this the Pope became enraged and proclaimed: 'O people of madmen! O the rejected ones! O foolish Talmudists!' After this outburst, another Jew, Don Todoros, spoke: 'O our Lord Pope, if the Talmudists are such fools in his eyes, why does he bring proofs from them to confirm that the Messiah has come? One does not bring proofs from madmen.' As the Pope grew even more furious another Jewish delegate protested: 'O lord Pope! It is not in accordance with the custom of his Holiness that he should be angry in matters of disputation; and permission was given to this extend; unless we have transgressed in some other way and have stumbled on our words – and for such an occasion we said "Show us our lord, your mercy".' (Maccoby, 1982, 177). As the debate unfolded the Jewish representatives became fearful that the scribes would falsify their remarks and later the Pope would say: 'You spoke thus!' – the result would then be that they would be convicted by their speech, and would not be able to call the

scribe a falsifier since he was well known to the Pope. As a result
the Jewish delegates agreed to be guarded in their speech and keep
silent as much as possible, yet this proved to be impossible since
the Pope ordered them to reply in every matter. To deal with this
danger, the Jews participating adopted the plan that only one of
them would speak; if his word pleased the Pope, they would
concur with what had been said, but if not, then they would say
that his reply was not the general view.

At one point in the disputation Rabbi Astruk jumped up and
said: 'O lord Pope! While you believe so many far-fetched things
about your Messiah, allow us to believe one about our Messiah!'
Fearful that this outburst would inflame the Pope's anger, the
Jewish delegates pleaded 'Out lord! Our colleague has not spoken
well, and entirely without our agreement. And he spoke by way of
jest – not that he had the right to do so'. When the Jews returned to
their lodgings they turned on Rabbi Astruk:

> 'Fie on you, and on your words, for you have put a sword in the
> hand of our enemies; and it is not according to our agreement
> that we should speak in the way you spoke. Our affairs were
> going well with the Pope, and he was more on our side than on
> Geronimo's; but now that the Pope has become angry, who will
> shield us, except the mercy of Heaven?'
>
> (Maccoby, 1982, 182)

Although the Tortosa Disputation gave Jewish delegates an opportunity to defend their views it was conducted in an atmosphere of
fear and impending disaster. As a consequence a large number of
Jews converted to the Christian faith and accepted baptism – they
gathered together in the hall of Assembly at Tortosa declaring
before the Jewish participants their acceptance of Christianity, and
once the disputation ended even more baptisms took place
including that of Don Vidal, the chief spokesman for the Jews in
the early part of the Disputation. The morale of Jewish–Christian
relations thus reached a low ebb. Faced with an alliance of the
church and the State, those who remained loyal to Judaism
regarded Christianity as a malevolent predator intent on uprooting
the Jewish heritage.

4

Persecution and Apostasy
in the Early Modern Period

As a consequence of Christian attempts to convert Spanish Jewry, a considerable number of Jews embraced the Christian faith. However in the fifteenth century the Church instituted a new form of persecution – under King Ferdinand and Queen Isabella the Inquisition was instructed to purge Jewish converts (Marranos) who were suspected of practising Jewish customs. Tribunals were established throughout the country which applied torture to extract confessions from the guilty. Seeking to escape such persecution, many Marranos sought refuge in Portugal where they led a Christian way of life while selectively observing Jewish practices. Following Spanish precedent however the Portuguese Inquisition was established in 1536 and attempted to track down Marranos wherever they lived. Other Marranos were driven to find homes in other lands where they returned to Judaism while retaining many of their former cultural characteristics. In such a milieu many of these individuals awaited the coming of the Messiah to lead them back to Zion, and in the seventeenth century a number of Marranos as well as others placed their hopes in the false Messiah, Shabbatai Tzevi, who eventually converted to Islam. Undeterred by this act of apostasy, a number of his followers continued to believe in him while embracing Islam. Subsequently a new Shabbatean sect emerged led by Jacob Frank who believed himself to be both the incarnation of Shabbatai Tzevi as well as the second person of the Trinity. Thus in the centuries following the Disputation of Tortosa Jewish life underwent considerable religious confusion as many Jews struggled to reconcile loyalty to their ancestral faith with pressures for conversion to Christianity as well as Islam.

MARRANOS

Following the Disputation of Tortosa, Pope Martin V decreed in 1421 and 1442 that forced baptism was not true baptism and condemned Jewish persecution. Under these more favourable conditions many of those who had converted to Christianity aspired to become full Jews again: this could be accomplished by moving to North Africa or Portugal. Yet this was not a solution open to all Jews, and those who remained in Spain baptized their children.

These Jewish converts kept apart from the Christian community; some were circumcised as adults. Such a return to Judaism was encouraged by the Fall of Constantinople to the Turks in 1453. This victory was seen by many Marranos as anticipating the fall of Edom and the deliverance of Israel. Thus in Valencia a group of Marranos, believing that the Messiah had just appeared on a mountain near the Bosphoros, sought to emigrate to Turkey. According to one of these converted Jews:

> The blind *goys* do not see that after we have been subject to them our God will now see to it that we dominate them. Our God has promised us that we will go to Turkey. We have heard that the Anti-Christ is coming; they say that the Turk is he, that he will destroy the Christian churches and will turn them into stables for the beasts and that he will bring honour and reverence to the Jews and the synagogues.
>
> (Poliakov, 1973, vol. 2, 173–4)

The practice of Judaism among the Marrano community was invariably adulterated as they sought to live Jewish lives in secret. Haunted by a sense of guilt, their prayers echoed such remorse:

> Lord, I have failed Thee by my meanness and my unworthiness, ruled by my evilness and by my treason in spite of myself. Thou, who hast visited me in true justice and hast cherished me like a son, see how I have fallen in a tribulation so great and so perilous, from which I cannot arise or escape. Knowing my guilt, I turn to Thee, Lord, repentant, sighing and weeping, as a son turns to his father, begging Thy holy mercy for forgiveness, that Thou mayest raise me from the great torment and the great tribulation into which I have fallen.
>
> (Poliakov, 1973, vol. 2, 174)

In order to free themselves from Christian allegiance, a number of Marranos attempted to de-Christianize themselves by following bizarre practices – fastening a crucifix to their buttocks, or destroying statues of Jesus. Others rationalized their duplicity. Thus the statesman and jurist Pedro de la Caballeria answered a Jewish scholar, who asked him how he could justify becoming a Christian, by pointing out the advantages of his new way of life: 'Imbecile,' he said, 'with the Jewish Torah what more could I have ever been than a rabbi? Now, thanks to the "little hanged one" I have been given all sorts of honours. I am in command of the whole city of Saragossa, and I make it tremble. What is there to keep me from fasting at Yom Kippur and observing your holidays if I feel like it? When I was Jew, I did not dare observe the Sabbath and now I do anything I want.'

Not all Marranos, however, sought to live such a double life; many become fervent Christians. Thus Fernán Pérez de Guzmán testified:

> I am going to put forward certain reasons to counter the opinion of those who, without distinction or difference, absolutely condemn that nation of New Christian converts of today, saying that they are not Christians and that their conversion was neither good nor useful... I believe that among them are people who are good and devoted, for the following reasons: first, I believe in the virtue of the holy baptismal water, which cannot be sprinkled and lavished without any result; second, I have known and I know good Marranos, who of their own free will lead an austere life in the religious orders; third, I have seen them work and wear themselves out in the monasteries, reforming dissolute and corrupt orders, and others, such as the honourable bishop (Paulus de Sancta Maria), and his honourable son don Alfonso, Bishop of Burgos, who have produced writings of great utility for our holy faith.
>
> (Poliakov, 1973, vol. 2, 176–7)

Yet even the Marranos who had become committed Christians were unable to escape their origins. Thus the poet Antonio de Montoro wrote to Queen Isabella at the time of her accession to the throne:

> I have said the Credo
> I have prayed to the pot of fat pork,
> I have heard Masses and I have prayed

And still have not been able to wipe out
The lineaments of a *confeso*.
I have prayed with devotion
And I have counted the beads
But I have never been able to lose
The name of a common old Jew.

(Poliakov, 1973, vol. 2, 176–7)

From the Christian side these Jewish apostates were despised because of their racial origins, despite the fact they had embraced the Church. The priest Andrés Bernáldez, for example, declared regarding their eating habits:

They never lose their Jewish way of eating, preparing their meat dishes with onions and garlic and cooking with oil, which they use in place of lard, so that they will not have to eat pork fat; and oil with meat is something which gives the breath a very bad odour; and their doorways smell very bad because of this way of cooking, and they themselves attribute their Jewish odour to these dishes.

(Poliakov, 1973, vol. 2, 84)

Such hostility to the Jewish converts was at times enshrined in official decrees. In 1449 the city officials of Toledo published a description of crimes committed by Marranos and proclaimed:

We declare that all the said *conversos* (Marranos), descendants of the perverse line of the Jews...in reason of the above-mentioned heresies and other offences, insults, seditions, and crimes committed by them up to this time, should therefore be held as disgraceful, unfit, inept, and unworthy of holding any office and public and private benefit in said city or public notaries or as witnesses... to have domain over Old Christians in the holy Catholic faith.

(Poliakov, 1973, vol. 2, 84)

THE INQUISITION AND THE MARRANOS

Under King Ferdinand and Queen Isabella the Inquisition came into full force, seeking to purge Marranos who were suspected of practising Jewish customs. In 1478 a papal bull was promulgated which established the Castilian Inquisition; four years later the first tribunal came into operation in Seville. Once the Inquisition was instituted, the tribunal requested that heretics give themselves up – this 'Edict of Grace' lasted for thirty days. Those who came forward to admit that they observed Jewish rites were obliged to denounce all other Judaizers. In compensation they were spared torture and imprisonment. Their sins were atoned for by flagellation, by wearing the *sembenito*, and by the confiscation of their belongings. In addition they were denied the right to hold office, practise a profession, or wear formal dress.

At the next stage of the Inquisitional process, Catholics were asked to name any suspects. An edict was promulgated which outlined various ways to recognize such individuals: Judaizers celebrated Jewish holidays, kept the dietary laws, consumed meat during Lent, omitted the phrase 'Glory be to the Father, and to the Son, and to the Holy Ghost' at the end of psalms, cooked with oil, and so forth. Once suspects were identified, the Inquisitors sought to obtain a confession. To achieve this end torture was used, interspersed with kind words such as: 'I pity you, when I see you so abused and with a lost soul...So do not assume the sin of others... admit the truth to me, for, as you see, I already know everything... In order that I may be able to pardon you and free you soon, tell me who led you to this error.' (Poliakov, 1973, vol. 2, 189)

Individuals who confessed saved their lives – those who persisted in denying the accusations made against them were burned at the stake. In this quest to root out heresy, there were some who even praised the execution of innocent victims. Thus in the sixteenth century Francesco Pegna stated: 'If an innocent is unjustly condemned, he has no reason to complain about the Church's sentence, which is based on sufficient proof, and what is hidden cannot be judged. If false witnesses have caused him to be condemned, he should accept the sentence with resignation, and rejoice in dying for truth.' (Poliakov,1973, vol. 2, 175) Although thousands of Jews died as martyrs, the majority of those who appeared before the Inquisition accepted reconciliation with the Church and were sentenced to imprisonment after undergoing various humiliations and having their property confiscated. In addition, their children and grandchildren were forbidden to wear gold or silver or hold public or ecclesiastical office.

The first tribunal was established in Seville where the majority of Marranos attempted to placate the Inquisitors by manifestations of Christian dedication as well as offerings and gifts. The rich

Marrano Mesa, for example, had the *quemadero* (the central place of atonement) decorated with statues of the prophets. None the less for seven years the Inquisition purged five thousand individuals who were punished and accepted reconciliation with the Church; seven hundred others were branded heretics and burned. In 1483, Tomas de Torquemada became Inquisitor for all of Spain, and tribunals were instituted in other provinces. In Aragon popular uprisings against the Inquisition took place; in Saragossa an attempt was made to assassinate the Inquisitor Pedro de Arbues. From 1486 to 1490 some 4850 Marranos were reconciled to the Church and fewer than two hundred burned.

Such zeal was defended by King Ferdinand even though he was aware of its economic implications. In response to the municipal authorities of Barcelona, who complained about the financial crisis the Inquisition had created, he answered: 'Before consenting to the establishment of the Inquisition in the cities of our kingdom, we considered the harm this could cause craftsmen and commerce. But in our great zeal for our holy faith, we have placed the service of the Lord well above all our other interests, whatever they may be.' Ironically, however, the Inquisition drove many Marranos back to their ancestral faith – in their distress they appealed to the God of Abraham, Isaac and Jacob. Defying Christ and Christianity, they declared the *Shema* ('Hear, O Israel, the Lord our God, the Lord is One') as they met their death. Some Catholics were also so disillusioned by the Inquisition that they converted to Judaism.

Jews who had never undergone baptism were frequently caught up in the coils of the Inquisition. The Inquisitors imposed the duty of identifying Judaizing Marranos, and charges were brought against those who attempted to convince baptized kinsmen to keep Jewish practices. In addition, those who promoted the return of Marranos to Judaism were indicted. Jews were also accused of engaging with Marranos in ritual murder. In 1490, six Jews and five Marranos of La Guardia were charged with attempting to destroy Christendom through black magic. According to the accusation made against one of the accused (Yuce Franco):

> His soul embittered and depraved, he went in good company with several others to crucify a Christian child on a Good Friday, in the same fashion, with the same animosity and cruelty as his forefathers had for our Saviour Jesus Christ, tearing his flesh, beating him and spitting in his face, covering him with wounds, crushing him with blows, and turning to ridicule our holy Faith...

He mixed its heart with a consecrated host. With this mixture, Yuce Franco and the others expected that the Christian religion would be overturned and destroyed, so that the Jews would possess all the property which belongs to the Catholics, that their race would grow and multiply while that of the faithful Christians would be extirpated forever.

(Poliakov, 1973, vol. 2, 196–7)

After confessions were obtained, all the accused were burned.

TORTURE AND EXILE

Torture during the Inquisition was designed to extract confessions from the guilty. When this end was achieved the Inquisitors were satisfied. Yet paradoxically, the innocent suffered more than those who practised Judaism in secret. An example of such suffering is reflected in a report on Elvira del Campo who was accused of not eating pork and wearing clean clothes on the Sabbath:

> She was carried to the torture chamber and told to tell the truth when she said that she had nothing to say. She was ordered to be stripped and again admonished, but was silent. When stripped, she said 'Senores, I have done all that is said of me and I bear false witness against myself, for I do not want to see myself in such trouble; please God, I have done nothing.' She was told not to bring false testimony against herself but to tell the truth. The tying of the arms was commenced. She said, 'I have told the truth; what have I to tell?' She was told to tell the truth and replied, 'I have told the truth and have nothing to tell.' One cord was applied to the arms and twisted, and she was admonished to tell the truth but said she had nothing to tell. Then she screamed and said, 'I have done all they say.'
>
> (Poliakov, 1973, vol. 2, 207)

The torture session then intensified, and according to rule more turns of the cord on the arm were applied.

> Another turn was ordered. She cried: 'Loosen me a little that I may remember what I have to tell, I don't know what I have done; I did not eat pork for it makes me sick; I have done

everything; loose me and I will tell the truth.' Another turn of the
cord was ordered...She was told to tell in detail truly what she
did. She said: 'What am I expected to tell? I did everything –
loosen me for I don't remember what I have to tell – don't you
see what a weak woman I am? Oh! Oh! my arms are breaking.'

(Poliakov, 1973, vol. 2, 207–8)

Once the sixteenth turn of the rope was administered, she was then
ordered to be placed on the *potro* (rack).

She said, 'Senores, why will you not tell me what I have to say?
Senor, put me on the ground – have I not said that I did it all?'
She was told to tell it. She said, 'I don't remember – take me
away – I did what the witnesses say.' She was told to tell me of
what I did not know – 'Senores, have mercy upon me – let me go
for God's sake – they have no pity on me – I did it – take me from
here and I will remember what I cannot here.'

She was told to state it, but replied, 'I don't know how to say it
– I have no memory – Lord, you are witness that if I knew how to
say anything else I would say it. I know nothing more to say than
that I did it and God knows it...The Law of which the witnesses
speak – I don't remember what Law it was – cursed be the
mother that bore me...Oh! Oh! they are killing me – if they
would tell me what – Oh, Senores! Oh my heart!'

(Poliakov, 1973, vol. 2, 208)

Many Spanish Marranos who sought refuge from the Inquisition
fled to Portugal. These crypto-Jews, unlike their Spanish counter-
parts, imitated the Christian way of life and complied with all
Catholic rites including attending mass and confession. None the
less they selectively observed various Jewish rituals and traditions
such as Yom Kippur and the Fast of Esther. In addition, they found
solace in Apocryphal texts, such as the Prayer of Esther which
became a central prayer of the Marranos: 'I whom you keep among
the infidels, you know how much I hate their criminal feasts...this
pomp to which I am condemned, this diadem in which I must
appear. Alone and in secret I trample them under my feet.' (Cohn-
Sherbok, 1992, 90)

Marrano insecurity frequently manifested itself in various
messianic movements. In the early sixteenth century, for example,
the adventurer David Reubeni presented himself to the court of

Pope Clement VII as a representative of a Jewish kingdom of the East. The Pope referred him to the King of Portugal where he sailed in a ship flying a Jewish flag. Marranos there were jubilant; their frenzy led them to attack the inquisitorial prison of Badajox. One of them, Diego Pires, became a Jew (taking the name Salomon Molcho) and joined Reubeni; together they travelled throughout Europe encouraging Messianic expectations. They were received by Charles V but finally were delivered to the Inquisition and burned at the stake.

The Inquisition was established in Portugal in 1536. Yet it was recognized that the New Christians constituted an important part of the population regardless of their religious beliefs and practices. Thus King John III informed the Pope that they greatly contributed to commerce and industry. They had served him well, he stated, and there was no reason to hate them. 'How can one dare to require me to cut the throats of my own flock?' he asked. (Poliakov, 1973, vol. 2, 238)

Nevertheless the Inquisition operated with fervour, tracking down Marranos in cities, villages, forests and mountains. As in Spain, Jewish martyrs went to their deaths with bravery. Thus after burning twenty New Christians in 1542, the Inquisitor of Lisbon praised their courage: 'Nothing astonished me so much as to see the Lord give such steadfastness to the weakness of flesh; children attended the burnings of their parents and wives those of their husbands and no one heard them cry out or weep. They said farewell and blessed them as if they were parting to meet again the next day.' (Poliakov, 1973, vol. 2, 240)

During this onslaught a number of Marranos fled abroad, but many remained behind to practise Judaism in secret. However, among these individuals knowledge of Judaism seriously declined, such that in an *auto da fé* in 1705 an archbishop declared: 'Miserable relics of Judaism! Unfortunate fragments of the synagogue! Last vestiges of Judea! Scandal for the Catholics, laughing-stock of the Jews themselves!...You are the laughing-stock of the Jews because you do not even know how to obey the law under which you live.' (Cohn-Sherbok, 1992) Although the distinction between New and Old Christians was eliminated at the end of the eighteenth century, Marranism continued to survive. Marranos continued to combine public Christian observances with secret Jewish rites; as they continued to observe certain Jewish holidays, they privately denied Christ whom they celebrated in church.

THE DISPERSION OF THE MARRANOS

The expulsion of Jews from Spain in 1492 drove thousands of Jews from Spain into Barbary, Turkey and the few Christians territories where they were allowed to settle. In the following two centuries Marranos continued to find homes abroad. In most cases these departures were facilitated through financial transactions, but in other instances they were the result of clandestine emigration. Thus in 1609–14 a number of Portuguese crypto-Jews and Spanish Marranos joined the Moriscos who had been expelled and crossed the Pyrenees.

In Turkey the Marranos were well received, since efforts had been made to attract them from the Iberian Peninsula ever since the conquest of Constantinople. At that time Sultan Mohammed II proclaimed: 'Here, descendants of the Hebrews who live in my country. Let each who desires it come to Constantinople, and let the remnant of your people find asylum here.' (Poliakov, 1973, vol. 2, 245) As a result many Jews fled to Constantinople, and by the middle of the sixteenth century a sizeable community had been established there. In the words of the French ambassador d'Aramon: 'Constantinople is inhabited principally by Turks, then by an infinite number of Jews, that is, Marranos who were driven out of Spain, Portugal and Germany. They have taught the Turks every handicraft, and the majority of the shops belong to Jews.' His contemporary Nicholas de Nicholay added:

> Among (the Jews) are very excellent workers in all arts and manufacturers, especially the Marranos who have recently been banished and chased from Spain and Portugal. To the great detriment and shame of Christianity, they have taught the Turks numerous inventions, artifices, and machines of war, such as how to make artillery, arquebuses, cannon powder, cannon balls, and other arms. Similarly, they have set up a printing shop, never before seen in these regions.
>
> (Poliakov, 1973, vol. 2, 246)

Salonica also constituted a Marrano refuge in the sixteenth century. The rabbis there encouraged them to become observant, yet among ordinary Jews they were often regarded with disapproval. Their ambiguous status led to considerable confusion: many Marranos did not know who they were and vacillated between Judaism and

Christianity. There were even those who returned to Judaism, and then out of longing for Christianity embraced the Christian faith. Others adopted Islam and served in the military under the Sultan.

Marranos settled in new countries for a variety of reasons. Some went to places where they could live freely as Jews; others were attracted by commercial and economic advantages. Aware of the financial contributions these newcomers could make, a number of Christian governments granted them special privileges. Yet wherever they went the Marranos remained Spanish in character and used Castilian written in Latin characters or Hebrew script to communicate with one another or for publishing their writings.

Such communal identification led to a feeling of disdain for German or Polish Jews. Thus in a letter to Voltaire, who was critical of Jews and Judaism, Isaac de Pinto wrote:

> M. Voltaire cannot be ignorant of the scrupulous exactness of the Portuguese and Spanish Jews not to intermix in marriage, alliance, or any other way, with the Jews of other nations...Their variance with their other brethren is such that if a Portuguese Jew in England or Holland married a German Jewess, he would of course lose all his prerogatives, be no long reckoned a member of their synagogue, forfeit all civil and ecclesiastical preferments, be absolutely divorced from the body of the nation, and not even be buried with his Portuguese brethren. This is the cause of those distinctions and of that elevation of mind which is observed among them, and which even their brethren of other nations seem to acknowledge.
>
> (Poliakov, 1973, vol. 2, 251)

Social cohesion among the Marrano community meant that even when returning to Judaism, they retained their former cultural characteristics. According to de Pinto, 'they do not wear beards, and do not affect any distinction in their clothing. Those who are well off pursue elegance and ostentation to the same extent as the other nations of Europe, from whom they differ only in religion.' (Cohn-Sherbok, 1992, 93) Such attitudes frequently led to criticism, such as that displayed by the preaching brother Labat who wrote of the Jews of Leghorn:

> They are free there, they do not wear any beard to distinguish them from the Christians. They are not confined to their neigh-

bourhoods. They are rich; their business is extensive. Almost all
have favours from the prince and they are protected to the point
where it is proverbial in Tuscany that it would be better to beat
the Grand Duke than a Jew. This only makes them all the more
odious to everyone else. But they laugh at this, and I do not
believe that there is any place in the world where they are more
arrogant and more haughty.

(Poliakov, 1973, vol. 2, 272)

Others, however, viewed these displaced Jews in a more favourable
light. Commenting on the Jews of Venice, the English navigator
Thomas Coryat wrote that they were

Such goodly and proper men, that I said to my selfe our English
proverbe To looke like a Jewe (whereby is meant sometimes a
weather beaten warp-faced fellow, sometimes a phrenticke and
lunaticke person, sometimes one discontented) is not true. For
indeed I noticed some of them to be most elegant and sweet
featured persons...I saw many Jewish women, whereof some
were as beautiful as ever I saw, and so gorgeous in their apparel,
jewels, chaines of gold, and rings adorned with precious stones,
that some of our English Countesses do scarce exceed them.

(Poliakov, 1973, vol. 2, 252)

The Marranos thus evoked differing responses from those among
whom they lived. Spanish by origin, outwardly Christian yet
Jewish by inclination, they despised their co-religionists. Not
surprisingly these contradictions frequently provoked profound
crises of personal identity and loyalty.

THE SHABBATEAN MOVEMENT

The story of the Marrano dispersion was linked to the Jewish expectation of the coming of the Messiah in the seventeenth century.
During this period Jewish believers, including many Marranos,
believed the coming of the Messiah was near at hand. In this milieu
the arrival of a self-proclaimed messianic king, Shabbatai Tzevi,
brought about a transformation of Jewish life. Born in Smyrna into a
Judeo-Spanish family, Shabbatai had received a traditional Jewish
education and later engaged in the study of the Zohar. After leaving

Smyrna in the 1650s he spent ten years in various cities in Greece as well as in Constantinople and Jerusalem. Eventually he became part of a kabbalistic group in Cairo and travelled to Gaza where he encountered Nathan Benjamin Levi who believed Shabbatai was the Messiah. In 1665 his messiahship was proclaimed and Nathan sent letters to Jews in the diaspora asking them to repent and recognize Shabbatai Tzevi as their redeemer. Shabbatai, he announced, would take the Sultan's crown, bring back the lost tribes, and inaugurate the period of messianic redemption. Throughout the entire dispersion, rich and poor made preparations to leave for Palestine.

After a brief sojourn in Jerusalem, Shabbatai went to Smyrna where he encountered strong opposition on the part of some local rabbis. In response he denounced the disbelievers and declared that he was the Anointed of the God of Jacob. This action evoked a hysterical response – a number of Jews fell into trances and had visions of him on a royal throne crowned as King of Israel. In 1666 he journeyed to Constantinople, but on the order of the Grand Vizier he was arrested and put into prison. Within a short time the prison chambers became a messianic court; pilgrims from all over the world made their way to Constantinople to join in messianic rituals and in ascetic activities. Hymns were written in his honour and new festivals were introduced. According to Nathan, who remained in Gaza, the alteration in Shabbatai's moods from illumination to withdrawal symbolized his soul's struggle with demonic powers: at times he was imprisoned by the powers of evil but at other moments he prevailed against them.

The same year Shabbatai spent three days with the Polish kabbalist, Nehemiah ha-Kohen, who later denounced him to the Turkish authorities. Shabbatai was brought to court and given the choice between conversion and death. In the face of this alternative, he converted to Islam and took on the name of Mehemet Effendi. Such an act of apostasy scandalized most of his followers, but he defended himself by asserting that he had become a Muslim in obedience to God's commands. Many of his followers accepted this explanation and refused to give up their belief. Some thought it was not Shabbatai who had become a Muslim, but rather a phantom who had taken on his appearance; the Messiah himself had ascended to Heaven. Others cited biblical and rabbinic sources to justify Shabbatai's action. Nathan explained that the messianic task involved taking on the humiliation of being portrayed as a traitor to his people.

After Shabbatai's act of apostasy, Nathan visited him in the Balkans and then travelled to Rome where he performed secret rites to bring about the end of the papacy. Shabbatai remained in Adrianople and Constantinople, where he lived as both Muslim and Jew. In 1672 he was deported to Albania, where he disclosed his own kabbalistic teaching to his supporters. After he died several years later, Nathan declared that Shabbatai had ascended to the supernal world. Eventually a number of groups continued in their belief that Shabbatai was the Messiah, including a sect, the Dissidents (*Doenmeh*), which professed Islam publicly but nevertheless adhered to their own traditions. Marrying among themselves, they eventually evolved into antinomian sub-groups which violated Jewish sexual laws and asserted the divinity of Shabbatai and their leader, Baruchiah Russo. In Italy several Shabbatean groups also emerged and propagated their views.

In the eighteenth century, the most important Shabbatean sect was led by Jacob Frank, who was influenced by the *Doenmeh* in Turkey. Believing himself to be the incarnation of Shabbatai, Frank announced that he was the second person of the Trinity and gathered together a circle of disciples who indulged in licentious orgies. In the 1750s, disputations took place between traditional Jews and Frankists; subsequently Frank expressed his willingness to become a Christian but he wished to maintain his own group. Although this request was refused by Church leaders, Frank and his disciples were baptized. The clergy, however, became aware that Frank's trinitarian beliefs were years. Frank then settled in Germany, where he continued to subscribe to a variant of the Shabbatean kabbalistic tradition.

5

The Impact of the Enlightenment

For the majority of European Jewry the medieval period extended into the eighteenth century, however the French Revolution followed by the Napoleonic period radically altered the status of the Jewish masses enabling them to enter into western life and culture. The spirit of emancipation unleashed by these events swept across Europe and freed Jews from their traditional lifestyle. The origins of Jewish thought during this period of change go back to seventeenth century Holland where a number of Jewish thinkers attempted to reevaluate Judaism in the light of current scientific developments. Preeminent among such writers was Baruch Spinoza who formulated a radical theological view which rejected the doctrine of a supernatural deity – distancing himself from any form of either Jewish Exclusivism or Inclusivism, he propounded a form of religious Pluralism consonant with the spirit of the age. In the following century the Jewish philosopher Moses Mendelssohn adopted a more traditional theological stance in which the Jewish people were viewed as the recipients of a divine revelation consisting of ritual and moral laws. Nonetheless, Mendelssohn believed that all peoples are capable of discerning God's reality through human reason: such a fusion of particularism and universalism constituted a modernist conception of Jewish Inclusivism. Two other thinkers of this period – Joseph Salvador and Abraham Geiger – similarly offered a sympathetic appreciation of another faith (Christianity) while at the same time adhering to the belief that Judaism is the superior religion.

THE EMANCIPATION OF JEWRY

In many respects the medieval period extended into the eighteenth century for the Jewish community. Despite the numerous changes taking place in European society, monarchs continued to rule by divine right. In addition the aristocracy was exempt from taxation and enjoyed special privileges; the established Church retained control over religious matters; and merchants and artisans closed ranks against outsiders. At the other end of the social scale peasants continued to be burdened with obligations to feudal masters, and in eastern and central Europe serfs were enslaved and exploited. By 1770 nearly two million Jews lived in this environment in Christian Europe. In some countries such as England and Holland they were relatively free from economic and social restrictions. The English and Dutch governments, for example, did not interfere with the private affairs and religious life of the Jewish population. Central European Jewry however was subject to a wide range of oppressive legal restrictions, and Jews were confined to special areas of residence. Furthermore Jews were forced to sew signs on their cloaks or wear special hats to distinguish them from their non-Jewish neighbours.

By the 1770s and 1780s the treatment of Jews in central Europe greatly improved due to the influence of such polemicists as Wilhelm Christian Dohm. In an influential tract, *Concerning the Amelioration of the Civil Status of the Jews*, Dohm argued that Jews did not pose any threat and could become valuable and patriotic citizens. A wise and benevolent society, he stressed, should abolish restrictions which prevent the Jewish population from having close contact with Christians and acquiring secular knowledge. All occupations, he argued, should be open to Jews and educational opportunities should be provided. The Holy Roman Emperor Joseph II echoed such sentiments. In 1781 he abolished the Jewish badge as well as taxes imposed on Jewish travellers; in the following year he issued an edict of toleration which granted Jews of Vienna freedom in trade and industry and the right of residence outside Jewish quarters. Moreover, regulations prohibiting Jews from leaving their homes before noon on Sunday and attending places of public amusement were abolished. Jews were also permitted to send their children to state schools or set up their own educational institutions. In 1784 Jewish judicial autonomy was abolished and three years later some Jews were inducted into the Hapsburg army.

As in Germany, reforms in France during the 1770s and 1780s ameliorated the situation of the Jewish population. Though Sephardic Jews in Paris and in the south and south-west lived in comfort and security, the Ashkenazic Jews of Alsace and Lorraine had a traditional Jewish lifestyle and were subject to a variety of disabilities. In 1789 the National Assembly issued a declaration proclaiming that all human beings are born and remain free and equal in rights and that no person should be persecuted for his opinions as long as they do not subvert civil law. In 1790 the Sephardim of south-west France and Jews from Papal Avignon were granted citizenship. This decree was followed in September 1791 by a resolution which granted citizenship rights to all Jews:

> The National Assembly, considering that the conditions requisite to be a French citizen, and to become an active citizen, are fixed by the constitution, and that every man who, being duly qualified, takes the civic oath, and engages to fulfil all the duties prescribed by the constitution, has a right to all the advantages it ensures – annuls all adjournments, restrictions and exceptions, contained in the preceding decrees, affecting individuals of the Jewish persuasion who shall take the civic oath.
>
> (Seltzer, 1980, 523)

This change in Jewish status occurred elsewhere in Europe as well – in 1796 the Dutch Jews of the Batavian republic were also granted full citizenship rights and in 1797 the ghettos of Padua and Rome were abolished.

In 1799 Napoleon became the First Consul of France and five years later he was proclaimed Emperor. Napoleon's Code of Civil Law propounded in 1804 established the right of all inhabitants to follow any trade and declared equality for all. After 1806 a number of German principalities were united in the French kingdom of Westphalia where Jews were granted the same rights. Despite these advances the situation of Jews did not undergo a complete transformation, and Napoleon still desired to regulate Jewish affairs. In July 1806 he convened an Assembly of Jewish Notables to consider a number of issues: Do Jewish marriage and divorce procedures conflict with French civil law? Are Jews allowed to marry Christians? Do French Jews consider Frenchmen their compatriots and is France their country?

In reply the Assembly decreed that Jewish law is compatible with French civil law; Jewish divorce and marriage are not binding unless preceded by a civil act; mixed marriage is legal but cannot be sanctioned by the Jewish faith; France is the homeland of French

Jews and Frenchmen should be seen as their kin. In the next year Napoleon summoned a Grand Sanhedrin consisting of rabbis and laymen to confirm the views of the Assembly. This body pledged its allegiance to the Emperor and nullified any features of the Jewish tradition that conflicted with the particular requirements of citizenship. In 1808 Napoleon issued two edicts regarding the Jewish community. In the first he set up a system of district boards of rabbis and laymen (consistories) to regulate Jewish affairs under the supervision of a central body in Paris. These consistories were responsible for maintaining synagogues and religious institutions, enforcing laws of conscription, overseeing changes in occupations ordered by the government and acting as a local police force. Napoleon's second decree postponed, reduced or abrogated all debts owed to Jews, regulated Jewish trade and residence rights and prohibited Jewish army conscripts from hiring substitutes.

BARUCH SPINOZA

The roots of Jewish thought during the Enlightenment go back to seventeenth century Holland where a number of thinkers attempted to view the Jewish tradition in the light of the new scientific conception of the world. In the previous century a revolution in scientific thought occurred with the publication of Copernicus' *Concerning Revolution of the Celestial Spheres*. This work broke with the Aristotelian science of the Middle Ages and inaugurated a fundamental shift in scientific theories of the universe. In place of the medieval belief that the earth was the centre of the cosmos, the new astronomy viewed the earth as in orbit around the sun. This altered picture of the heavens was far more successful in predicting the behaviour of heavenly bodies; the motion of all bodies could on this basis be described in simple mathematical ratios. As a result, the cosmos was conceived as ruled by invariable and uniform laws.

Within Judaism the first symptoms of this new scientific world view appeared in seventeenth-century Amsterdam where Spanish and Portuguese Marranos had fled from the Inquisition. Prominent among Jewish thinkers was Uriel Acosta who rejected the doctrine of immortality as well as the authority of the rabbis. Excommunicated by the Amsterdam Jewish community, he later underwent a public renunciation of his opinions and later committed suicide. Toward the end of his life, Acosta came to the view that the Torah was not divine in origin since 'it concerns many things contrary to natural law; and God, the creator of nature, cannot possibly have contradicted himself, which would have been the case had he given to men rule of obedience contrary to the first law'. (Acosta, 1967, 18–19).

Echoing Acosta's radical departure from tradition, the Dutch Jewish philosopher, Baruch Spinoza espoused unorthodox religious beliefs. Condemned by the Orthodox authorities, he was excommunicated and expelled from the Jewish community. In the remaining years of his life, he lived in various towns and attracted a circle of disciples. In 1670 he published the *Tractatus Theologico-Politicus* in which he rejected the medieval synthesis of faith and reason. In the first part of this work, he argued that the prophets possessed moral insight rather than theoretical truth. Rejecting the Maimonidean belief that the Bible contains a hidden esoteric meaning, Spinoza argued that the Hebrew Scriptures were intended for the masses. God, he continued, is conceived as a lawgiver to appeal to the multitude; the function of Biblical law was to ensure social stability. In addition Spinoza asserted that God cannot be known through miraculous occurrences but only from the order of nature and clear self-evident ideas. As far as the Torah is concerned, it was not composed in its entirety by Moses – the historical books were compilations assembled by many generations. Ezra, he believed, was responsible for harmonizing the discrepancies found in Scripture.

For Spinoza the function of religion is to provide a framework for ethical action. Philosophy on the other hand is concerned with truth, and philosophers should be free to engage in philosophical speculation unconstrained by religious opinions:

Faith, therefore allows the greatest latitude in philosophical speculation, allowing us without blame to think what we like about anything, and only condemning, as heretics and schismatics, those who teach opinions which tend to produce obstinacy, hatred, strife, and anger while, on the other hand, only considering as faithful those who persuade us, as far as their reason and faculties will permit, to follow justice and charity.

(Spinoza, 1951, 189)

It is a usurpation of the social contract and a violation of the rights of man to legislate belief. On the basis of this view Spinoza propounded a metaphysical system based on a pantheistic conception of nature. Beginning with the belief in an infinite, unlimited, self-caused Substance which he conceived as God or nature, Spinoza maintained that Substance possesses a theoretical infinity of attributes, only two of which – extension and thought – are apprehended by human beings. God or nature can also be seen as a whole made up of finite, individual entities. In this way God exists in all things as their universal essence; they exist in God as modifications.

This philosophical scheme was based on Spinoza's concept of three grounds of knowledge. The lowest form depends on sense perception – it consists of ideas which are linked by association. Such an apprehension is of practical value, yet it is inadequate because it does not involve an understanding of both the reason and cause of things. The second grade consists of systematic knowledge such as mathematics in which propositions are deduced from axioms and postulates. In the seventeenth century the laws of science and physics were of this nature: in his *Ethics* Spinoza utilized such a framework – based on Euclid's geometry – to arrange the truth of consciousness into a rigorously logical system. The highest level of knowledge is intuitive reason based on scientific and logical thinking which can comprehend the interconnection of the whole. The person who reaches this final stage is able to apprehend reality as a unity and attain the love of God through knowledge:

> The wise man...is scarcely at all disturbed in spirit, but being conscious of himself, and of God, and of things, by a certain eternal necessity...always possesses true acquiescence of his spirit. If the way which I have pointed out as leading to this result seems exceedingly hard, it may nevertheless be discovered. Needs must it be hard, since it is so seldom found. How would it be possible, if salvation were ready to our hand, and could without great labour be found, that it should be by almost all men neglected? But all things excellent are as difficult as they are rare.
>
> (Spinoza, 1951, vol. 2, 270–1)

According to Spinoza, God is the sum of the laws of nature – he is totally immanent. Further, Spinoza argued that God is not incorporeal; instead he is the totality of all bodies in the universe. On this view creation is ruled out and the whole is free only to the degree that it is self-caused. When one submits to the logical and necessary connection of reality, it is possible to attain tranquillity and a liberation from trivial concerns.

In propounding these views Spinoza was not concerned with the relationship between the Jewish faith and other religions, yet his rejection of the authority of the Bible and his espousal of pantheism had important ramifications for later Jewish thought. Breaking with biblical and rabbinic Judaism, Spinoza rejected the traditional Jewish belief that God created the universe, chose the Jews, delivered them from Egyptian bondage and revealed the Law to Moses on Mount Sinai. For Spinoza God is not a supernatural deity in the traditional sense – rather he is the totally immanent aggregate of natural laws. As such he does not act in history, reveal himself to any particular people, or exercise a providential influence on the course of events. Spinoza's theology is thus far removed from both Jewish Exclusivism and Inclusivism of the biblical and rabbinic periods; instead his pantheistic ideas implicitly presuppose a form of religious Pluralism, shaped by scientific thought in the early modern period, in which all religions (including Judaism) are conceived as imperfect and erroneous human attempts to discern the nature of divine reality.

MOSES MENDELSSOHN

The principles of rational inquiry advanced by Spinoza and others in the seventeenth century continued to dominate the cultural climate of the following century. During the period of the Enlightenment political and religious reformers advocated the application of human reason to all spheres of inquiry. From France this spirit of rationalism spread throughout Europe and to the United States. In Germany the Jewish thinker Moses Mendelssohn spearheaded a revaluation of traditional Jewish religious life and thought. Born in Dessau as the son of a Torah scribe, Mendelssohn received a traditional Jewish education but became increasingly preoccupied with secular learning. In the 1750s he befriended the dramatist and literary critic Gotthold Ephraim Lessing who was the leading advocate of enlightened toleration in Germany.

Prior to their acquaintance, Lessing had written a play portraying a Jew of exceptional qualities – for both Lessing and other liberal thinkers Mendelssohn represented such a figure. With Lessing's encouragement Mendelssohn published a series of essays in which he argued for the existence of God and creation, and he propounded the view that human reason is able to discover the reality of God, divine providence, and the immortality of the soul. At the height of his career, Mendelssohn was challenged by a Christian apologist to explain why he remained a Jew. From 1769 he defended Judaism, and in 1783 published *Jerusalem, or On Religious Power and Judaism*. In this study Mendelssohn contended that no religious institutions should use coercion; neither the Church nor the state, he believed, has the right to impose its religious views on the individual. Addressing the question as to whether the Mosaic law sanctions such coercion, Mendelssohn stressed that Judaism does not coerce the mind through dogma:

> The Israelites possess a divine legislation – laws, commandments, statutes, rules of conduct, instruction in God's will and in what they are to do to attain temporal and eternal salvation. Moses in a miraculous and supernatural way, revealed to them these laws and commandments, but not dogmas, propositions concerning salvation, or self-evident principles of reason. These the Lord reveals to us and as well to all other men at all times through nature and events, but never through the spoken or written word.
> (Mendelssohn, 1969, 61)

The distinction Mendelssohn drew between natural religion and the Jewish faith was based on three types of truth: logically necessary truth, contingent truths such as the laws of nature, and the temporal truths that occur in history. In this connection, he wrote: 'Whenever God intends man to understand a certain truth, his wisdom provides man with the means most suited to this purpose. If it is a necessary truth, God provides man with whatever degree of reason he requires for its understanding. If a natural law is to be disclosed to man, God's wisdom will provide him with the necessary capacity for observation; and if a historical truth is to be presented for posterity, God's wisdom authenticates its historicity by establishing the narrator's credibility beyond any doubt.' (Mendelssohn, 1969, 64–5).

According to Mendelssohn, all human beings have the innate capacity to discover the existence of God, providence and the hereafter. But Judaism is uniquely different from other religions in that it contains a revealed law. The Jewish people did not hear God proclaim that he is an eternal, necessary, omnipotent and omniscient being who rewards and punishes humanity: instead divine commandments were revealed to God's chosen people:

> The voice that was heard at Sinai on the great day did not proclaim, 'I am the eternal, your God, the necessary autonomous being, omnipotent and omniscient, who rewards men in a future life according to their deeds.' This is the universal religion of mankind not Judaism, and this kind of universal religion – without which man can become neither virtuous nor happy – was not and, in fact, could not have been revealed at Sinai. For who could have needed the sound of thunder and the blast of trumpets to become convinced of the validity of these eternal verities?
>
> (Mendelssohn, 1969, 68–9)

Rather at Mount Sinai the Jewish people heard the historical truth 'I am the Lord your God who brought you out of the land of Egypt' – a statement introducing the legal code which is binding on the Jewish nation.

For Mendelssohn the purpose of ceremonial law is to bring all peoples to a belief in ethical monotheism:

> And now I am finally at the point where I can elucidate my hypothesis about the purpose of the ceremonial law in Judaism. Our people's patriarchs – Abraham, Isaac, and Jacob – had remained faithful to the Eternal and tried to preserve pure religious concepts free of all idolatry, for their families and descendants. And now these descendants were chosen by Providence to be a nation of priests, that is, a nation which, through its constitution and institutions, through its laws and conduct, and throughout all changes of life and fortune, was to call wholesome and unadulterated ideas of God and his attributes continuously to the attention of the rest of mankind. It was a nation which through its mere existence, as it were, would unceasingly teach, proclaim, preach and strive to preserve these ideas among the nations.
>
> (Mendelssohn, 1969, 89)

Yet despite this universal mission, Jews are not at liberty to divorce themselves from their cultural connections with the countries where they dwell. Rather they must engage in civic life while remaining faithful to their religious heritage:

Adopt the mores and constitution of the country in which you find yourself, but be steadfast in upholding the religion of your fathers, too. Bear both burdens as well as you can. True, on the one hand, people make it difficult for you to bear the burden of civil life because of the religion to which you remain faithful; and, on the other hand, the climate of our time makes the observance of your religious laws in some respects more burdensome than it need be. Persevere nevertheless; stand fast in the place which Providence has assigned everything which may happen, as you were told to do by your Lawgiver long ago.

(Mendelssohn, 1969, 104–5)

At the end of *Jerusalem*, Mendelssohn argued for the individuality of all religious traditions. Rejecting the idea that all faiths should be merged into one universal creed, he maintained that the existence of many different religions is fundamental: 'Brothers, if you care for true godliness, do not pretend that conformity exists where diversity is obviously the plan and goal of Providence' (Mendelssohn, 1969, 104–5). In Mendelssohn's view then human reason serves as a means by which all people can arrive at universal truths about the nature of God and his activity in the world. In this sense all religions have the capacity to discover the reality of God, divine providence, and the immortality of the soul. Yet as far as Judaism is concerned, the Jewish people are the recipients of a divine revelation consisting of ritual and moral law. This supernatural dispensation is what distinguishes Judaism from other faiths, and serves to impel the nation toward their universal mission for all humanity. By fusing universalism and particularism in this fashion, Mendelssohn argued for a form of Jewish Inclusivism consistent with the rationalist spirit of the eighteenth century.

JOSEPH SALVADOR

During the period of the Enlightenment the French Jewish thinker Joseph Salvador undertook an evaluation of Christianity from a Jewish perspective. Professionally trained as a doctor, Salvador's interest in Judaism was evoked by the anti-Semitic riots which took place in Germany in 1819. In his early words (*La Loi de Moise* and *Histoire des institutions de Moise et du peuple Hebreux*) he described Moses as a founder of the first republic; according to Salvador, such an accomplishment should entitle Jews to human and civil rights. In addition to these studies Salvador sought to depict Jesus in the context of first century Judaism: his study of Jesus was first published in France and subsequently translated into German.

Throughout this work Salvador focused on the historical background of the Gospels. In the preface he stressed his intention to present an impartial investigation of the origin of the Christian faith:

> The first books shall be dedicated to an exposition of the favourable circumstances which led to the formation of Christianity; it is an introduction which shall concern itself with these questions in its three chapters: the earliest historical origin and respective position of various nations at the time of the arrival of the son of Mary; ...to discover the nature of the pattern whose most significant result was Christianity. Further to determine the condition of the intellectual and spiritual position of the upper and lower classes of the Oriental and Greek people. Finally to discover all the indispensable details of the land which was the cradle of Christianity, to which it owes its first plans, its early apostles, and its first language; and to ascertain as well the difference among the various Hebrew schools of thought which were diffused in Judea as well as the Diaspora.
>
> (Salvador, 1841, 5ff)

Such an approach constituted a major departure from the romanticism of mid-nineteenth century studies of Jesus undertaken by Christian scholars which largely neglected the Jewish dimensions of the New Testament world.

According to Salvador, the Gospel of Matthew is the best and earliest source, whereas the Fourth Gospel represents the last stage in the development of early Christianity. Unlike other writers (such as the Christian scholar David Friedrich Strauss), Salvador was uninterested in textual criticism; instead he began by asking whether Jesus had ever lived. Rejecting the view that the stories of Jesus are mere fantasy, Salvador argued that the Gospels reveal a real historical figure despite the discrepancies in the various accounts. For Salvador the silence of Jewish sources about Jesus is not an obstacle to believing that Jesus existed – the oral tradition of Christianity, he stressed, should be regarded as reliable just as is the oral testimony within Judaism. Yet although Salvador accepted the historicity of Jesus, he was sceptical of several Christian doctrines connected with Jesus' life. Concerning belief in Immaculate Conception, for example, Salvador focused on the few facts known about Joseph and Mary. Whatever may have taken place, he argued, it appears that the couple escaped to Egypt to avoid rumours about their relationship. By eliminating the mythic elements of the story, Salvador sought to provide a rational reconstruction of events.

Salvador was also anxious to distinguish between those features of Christianity attributable to Jesus as opposed to those stemming from John the Baptist. John the Baptist, he asserted, had combined together elements of the divergent streams of thought within first century Judaism. 'So the foundation of a new Jewish school was undertaken,' he wrote, 'It developed from the union of the genuine, but different Essene morality with the keen missionary zeal of the Pharisees.' (Salvador, 1841, 120). The teachings of John the Baptist were subsequently transformed by Jesus: 'In the person of Jesus a new combination was formed; it joined the moral elements of the land of Israel with the highest form of the Oriental doctrine of resurrection, which the captive tribes had brought with them from Babylonia and Persia.' (Salvador, 1841, 121). In his teaching Jesus personified Scripture and through his resurrection transferred them to the world to come.

In propagating this view, Salvador stressed that the hostility between Jesus and the Pharisees is an historical fact. According to the testimony of his own chroniclers, Jesus sought to defeat his opponents in the cities and countryside as well as in synagogues and even in the Temple precincts. The conflicts between Jesus and the Pharisees were events of history. The New Testament, he argued, illustrates that Jesus 'wandered freely through the land, spoke, preached, and sought to defeat his opponents everywhere – in the cities, in the countryside, in the Pharisaic synagogues, and even in the very precincts of the Temple.' (Salvador, 1841, 329). Later when Jesus committed blasphemy as defined by Pharisaic Judaism, Salvador continued, he must have realized that he might incur the death penalty as a result – from this perspective his death should be viewed as part of his destiny and the starting point of the Christian faith:

The historic and continuing guiding principle of the activities and statements of Mary's son remains his death. He had contemplated it far in advance...It led to the quick success of his promises among the foreign masses.

(Salvador, 1841, 314)

In espousing this thesis Salvador focused on Jesus' trial. Here he discussed the involvement of Jewish authorities, claiming that the decree of the tribunal was justified since Jesus was guilty of blaspheming against the tradition. Regarding the involvement of the Romans, Salvador pointed out that the execution itself was left to the Romans since only they were empowered to carry out this verdict. Furthermore, he maintained that the Romans had their own motives in executing Jesus: the political implications of his activities caused considerable alarm.

Regarding Jesus' mission, Salvador declared that Jesus' life demanded such a death. Since he had been unable to accomplish his purposes on earth:

It is certain that the personal plan of the son of Mary failed; he wished through his words to unite the different schools of the Hebrew people. He sought to articulate their hopes in the dogma expressed by him, but neither before nor after his death was this realized. His struggle with Pharisaism was never crowned by a decisive victory.

(Salvador, 1841, 368)

In consequence Jesus' followers transformed his image from that of an historical figure to a symbol – the character of Jesus became a mythological personality under the influence of Oriental mysticism. The Jesus of history became the Christ of faith.

With reference to Jesus' teaching, Salvador stressed that through-out his life Jesus continually relied on his ancestral tradition: in the sphere of ethics the only distinction lay in Judaism's emphasis on society as opposed to Jesus' concern with the individual. As far as the world-to-come is concerned, Jesus was intent in viewing earthly life as a momentary interlude in the eternal scheme:

His life, and his soul did not rest upon the freedom or the positive happy aspects of this world; in his eyes those remained the special realm of Satan. This world was an old, vanishing phantom, which would have to be replaced by a new creation.

(Salvador, 1841, 218)

In Salvador's opinion such other-worldliness had a profound effect on later Christian thought; throughout its history, he believed, the Church has turned away from social and political reformation due to its negation of this-worldly concerns.

Continuing this discussion of the development of Christianity, Salvador argued that the apostles added pagan elements to the teachings of Jesus in order to adapt their faith to an Oriental milieu. In this transformation, Paul was instrumental. 'Paul,' he wrote, 'was a many-sided, cultured man who became the leader of the second phase, or the second school, of Christianity. The symbol of Jesus Christ left the national sphere to serve broader society through its personification. This was done at his command. After a long struggle with the Christians of the first school and with practically all the apostles, including Peter, he forced them to abandon the point of view of the Synagogue and the Jewish schools. He induced them to establish a separate entity, the Church. In this way the division of the Jewish people into two parts occurred; they became Jews and Christians.' (Salvador, 1841, 374).

The final phase of the early Church was introduced by the apostle John:

> Paul made a new Adam of Jesus...The apostle John evoked another figure...that of the heavenly Adam, a figure through which the doctrine of the Trinity would be further enhanced... From that moment on the apostle saw something completely different from a moral force or a moral type in his teacher. He was more than a living instrument of wisdom through which society would be improved, or who would provide specific laws to improve the discernment of the conscience. His Gospel recognized in the son of Mary the immediate cause and creator of the world.
>
> (Salvador, 1841, 480)

In this pioneering study Salvador broke with the medieval Jewish past in which Jews lived in fear of their Christian neighbours. Instead of recoiling from Christianity, Salvador sought to understand its origin and development. With sympathy and understanding he discussed its Jewish roots and introduction of Jewish ideas into the world. Yet his analysis was not uncritical; for Salvador in its evolution Christianity had lost many of its Jewish elements. In a later work he wrote:

With regard to the unity of God, which his teaching proclaims, all the errors of polytheism are hallowed by it. In respect to religious equality, of which it has been very proud, one must point out that the inequality of castes has been vastly increased. Poverty, which is no less terrible for the physical man, has had innumerable apologists who have spoken from its altars heaped with gold and riches.

(Salvador, 1860, vol. 2, 473 ff)

Despite these difficulties however Salvador believed that in the future Christians would help to bring about a new philosophical religion which would resemble Judaism – in this respect his positive evaluation of the Christian past and future provided a form of Jewish Inclusivism tempered by the scientific spirit of the period of the Enlightenment.

ABRAHAM GEIGER

One of the most important Jewish reformers during the Enlightenment was Abraham Geiger who combined a commitment to the scientific study of Judaism with a rabbinic career. Born in Frankfurt, Geiger studied at the Universities of Heidelberg and Bonn; in 1832 he served as a rabbi in Wiesbaden where he edited the *Scientific Journal for Jewish Theology*. In 1838 he was appointed rabbi in Breslau where he published studies on a variety of Jewish subjects as well as a book on the ancient text and translations of the Bible. In this work Geiger maintained that post-biblical Jewish movements shaped the canonized version of Scripture. Although Geiger did not write a systematic Jewish theology, his approach was based on a programme to reformulate Judaism in order to achieve theological clarity according to the scientific spirit of the time. For Geiger religion is rooted in the human recognition of finitude and the quest for the infinite. Judaism, he believed, is 'a faith founded on the trust in one who guides the universe and in the task imposed upon us to practise justice and manifest in acts that fulfil this demand, and that is clothed in uplifting ritual forms designed to awaken such sentiments'. (Cohn-Sherbok, 1987, 145). Unlike the Greeks who believed in fate, the Jewish faith conceives spiritual perfection as the ultimate aim of human striving. According to Geiger this vision which reached its climax in the prophetic tradition should be

distinguished from earlier, more primitive religious practices such
as animal sacrifice which had been discarded in the course of Jewish
history. Similarly he argued that the biblical concept of nationhood
is not needed in the modern world.

For Geiger the evolution of Jewish history is divided into four
stages of development. First in the age of revelation, the idea of
Judaism was seen as a moral, spiritual concept capable of continual
development. In the second stage of Jewish history – the age of
tradition – the Bible was continually reshaped and reinterpreted.
The third stage – the age of legalism – which occurred after the
completion of the Talmud, formalized the tradition so as to ensure
its continuance. Finally, in the age of critical study, legalism was
transcended through historical research. Yet, though the *halakhah*
was not considered binding in the fourth stage, this does not imply
that Judaism is cut off from the past; on the contrary historical
studies can revitalize the heritage. Those aspects of the Jewish
tradition which are to be eliminated should be regarded as
medieval abnormalities resulting from restraints – they are not
connected to the core of the Jewish faith.

In his writing, Geiger was also anxious to understand the Jewish
background of Christianity and thereby combat the anti-Semitic
tendencies of eighteenth century New Testament scholarship.
According to Geiger, Jesus 'was a Jew, a Pharisee Jew with some
Galilean colourations; he was an individual who shared the hopes
of his time and believed that this hope had been fulfilled in him. He
uttered no new thoughts nor did he break through the boundaries
of nationalism'. (Geiger, 1910, 118f). Following the tradition of
Hillel, Jesus fitted into the context of first century Palestine.
Although he considered himself to be the Messiah, such a claim
was in no sense heretical. Jesus' life and thought thus were
authentically Jewish with the possible exception of his views about
demons and resurrection. Given such a conception of Jesus, Geiger
concluded that:

> We cannot deny him a deep introspective nature, but there is no
> trace of a decisive stand that promised lasting results...there was
> no great work of reform nor any new thoughts that left the usual
> paths. He did oppose abuses, perhaps occasionally more force-
> fully than the Pharisees, yet on the whole it was done in their
> manner.
>
>   (Geiger, 1875, vol. 2, 113f)

According to Geiger, Jesus believed that a new world of history had been inaugurated in his lifetime, and his followers awaited the new age. Regarding Paul, Geiger argued that he was deeply influenced by Hellenistic Judaism and Philo's concept of the Logos – in his teaching Paul transformed the original messianic sect in which Jesus was conceived as the intermediary between God and humanity.

Jesus as well as early Christianity was also influenced by the Sadducees. 'The High Priesthood of Jesus,' Geiger wrote, 'his death as a sacrifice, the participation in the eucharist with his blood and body became a new priesthood endowed with the sacredness and holiness of the old.' (Geiger, 1874, 15ff). According to Geiger, the Judeo-Christian sect eventually began to spread its message to gentiles. The first stage of its development was essentially Jewish – this period was represented by the original version of the Gospel of Mark. A later version contained the expression 'Son of God' which was later used by other gospel writers – this marked the second stage in the evolution of the Church:

> In the second stage of its development and through it, Christianity almost ceased to be a path within Judaism despite all efforts to maintain itself within Judaism.
>
> (Geiger, 1910, 130ff)

According to Geiger, Christianity's final break with its Jewish past was initiated by Paul who had been influenced by Hellenistic Jewish thought with its emphasis on the Messiah and the Logos. This initiative gained impetus with the destruction of the Temple and the defeat of Bar Kokhba.

In his *Introduction to Jewish Theology* Geiger explored the impact of Christianity on civilization. The strength of the Christian faith, he believed, consists in its struggle against human nature and its quest to unite all peoples. Yet, he argued, its strength is also its weakness: in its pursuit to draw non-Christians to Christ, Christianity has destroyed the civilizations of the ancient world. In addition, the Church has been overly preoccupied with preserving its power, and has frequently endeavoured to subdue human reason. Judaism on the other hand, has never been burdened by such concerns. For this reason it is the superior religion:

> Judaism is self-sufficient, developed out of its own resources and may abandon the outer garb of a particular period without

surrendering anything of its essence; Christianity, on the other hand, rests upon the configuration of the Judaism of a particular period and must eternally cling to what appeared at that particular time in the historical flow of life; for it these elements must remain eternally complete.

(Jacob, 1974, 47)

Moreover, for Geiger Christianity is the inferior religion since the doctrine of the Incarnation compromised the original purity of the Jewish covenant of God. Further, Geiger asserted that the concept of original sin undermines the biblical view that human beings are capable of moral improvement. Geiger also pointed out that the validity of Judaism does not rest on a historical figure like Jesus. Finally Geiger emphasized that Judaism does not contain fixed dogma which constrain free inquiry. For these reasons Geiger believed that Judaism rather than the Christian faith is the ideal system for the modern age:

For to speak plainly, the modern is not Christian and the Christian is not modern...Modern culture leans in religion upon Jewish monotheism and in sciences and arts on Hellenism, while it either ignores or rejects the specifically Christian.

(Geiger, 1911, 392)

In various writings then Geiger acknowledged Christianity's debt to Judaism. The Christian faith he believed, embraces God's revelation to his chosen people, yet by distorting God's true message it has ceased to be a viable force in modern life.

6
Jewish Reflections in the Age of Emancipation

Once emancipated, Jewish thinkers began to grapple with the main currents of Western philosophical thought and in their different ways offered a positive evaluation of both Christianity and Islam of Western philosophical thought. Pre-eminent among mid-nineteenth century Jewish writers, Samuel Hirsh argued that throughout history Judaism sought to overcome the threat of paganism. In this quest, he believed, Christianity has a role, yet ultimately it is the Jewish faith – as the purest form of monotheism – which is humanity's hope for the future. A similar position was espoused by Solomon Formstecher who maintained that Judaism is the ultimate form of the religious life; nonetheless, he stressed, both Christianity and Islam as monotheistic faiths play a role in the unfolding of God's plan. A third figure of this period, Solomon Ludwig Steinheim also viewed Christianity as furthering God's eschatological scheme; although inferior to Judaism the Christian faith serves as a means of accomplishing God's purposes. In contrast with these thinkers, Hermann Cohen was severely critical of Christian theology, however he too pleaded for a better relationship between Christianity and Judaism in the struggle to bring knowledge of one God to all people. Such qualified endorsements of Christianity were superseded by Claude Montefiore's attempt to present Christianity in the most positive light. According to Montefiore, God reveals himself in different ways throughout history – the Christian faith, he stressed, is one such disclosure and Jews can be enlightened by a knowledge of the New Testament.

SAMUEL HIRSCH

In the mid-nineteenth century Jewish thinkers were confronted by the challenge of three major philosophers: Kant, Schelling and

Hegel. In their different ways each of these German thinkers was preoccupied with the role of religion (in particular Christianity) in society. In response Samuel Hirsch, a German rabbi who had participated in the creation of Liberal Judaism, published *The Religious Philosophy of the Jews* in 1842 in which he attempted to demonstrate Judaism's superiority over Christianity.

Influenced by Hegelian thought, Hirsch argued that human beings become aware of their freedom by seeing themselves as distinct selves over and against the world. Yet, he departed from Hegel in one central aspect. For Hegel, primary, abstract freedom leads eventually to actual, concrete freedom when human beings discover that they are finite beings rooted in nature yet destined for reason. According to Hegel this is the philosophical meaning of the human awareness of sin: sin can be overcome only when this dialectically necessary contradiction is resolved through rational self-determination. Hirsch however argued that sin is a moral rather than intellectual state. Sin is thus inherent in the ability to choose between alternatives and can be overcome only through moral activity. Thus Hirsch believed the essential content of religion is not the self-realization of God, but the actualizing of human moral freedom. As a divine gift, such freedom gives rise to the task of subordinating natural sensuality to ethical responsibility.

For Hirsch there are two types of religion: passive religion and active religion. In passive religion freedom is renounced and human beings are dominated by sensual desires – in such cases nature is elevated to an all-powerful divine force. According to Hirsch such paganism is not even partially valid because in the course of history pagan consciousness will ultimately come to realize its futility. In active religion on the other hand human beings are capable of rising to the level of self-chosen freedom in realizing that this is God's desire. Judaism, Hirsch believed, possessed the insight of active religion from the time of the patriarchs. Further, the miracles as well as prophecies of the Bible were historically necessary in order to eliminate a residue of paganism among the Jewish people. However, the need for most miracles has ceased – the only permanent miracle in Jewish history is the survival of the Jewish people itself.

On this view Hirsch criticized Hegel's contention that Judaism is only a partial truth which has been superseded by the religious consciousness of Protestant Christianity. In Judaism, he maintained, there is no evolution of religious truth; development consists in the ethical education of Jewry. The purpose of such instruction is to ensure that all Jews embody intensive religiosity by choosing virtue rather than sin. Further, the Jewish nation has the task of bringing humanity closer to divine truth by acting as God's suffering servant. Christianity too has a role in the unfolding of God's plan: it is the task of the Church to bring true religious consciousness to pagans.

In explaining this mission, Hirsch explored the nature of the gospel witness. Like other nineteenth-century scholars, he drew a distinction between the Jesus of the Synoptic Gospels and the Fourth Gospel. Although Christian faith has favoured the abstract Jesus of the Fourth Gospel, Hirsch believed modern Christianity should stress the historical Jesus of the Synoptic Gospels: in this way Jesus could be understood as a real flesh-and-blood person rather than an abstract ideal. Such an historical personage is, he believed, of relevance to the Jewish community and to all human kind:

> Every Jew, for that matter every man, should be what Jesus was; that was the summons of every prophet. Every Jew and every man will become so; that is the promise of the Messianic hope.
>
> (Hirsch, 1842, 728)

Hirsch considered Jesus' major contribution to have been the renewal of the prophetic voice: 'At the time of Jesus' appearance, Judaism had forgotten the source of its truth. The voices of living prophets had long faded away.' (Hirsch, 1854, 224). Jesus thus directed his words to fellow Jews because he desired to make the goal of all Israel meaningful for each individual. Instead of intending to create a new religion, he sought to realize the total content of the old.' (Hirsch, 1842, 689).

The development of Christianity into a new religion did not occur through Jesus. Hirsch insisted instead that Jesus stood firmly within the Jewish tradition: 'All that he taught, as he himself admitted, had already been given by Moses and the prophets. He did not die for an idea; nor did he leave his disciples a legacy independent of his person. The unusual attainment of Jesus lay in something that was far more than an idea, it lay in his personality. He understood, realized, and fulfilled the idea of Judaism in its deepest truth – that was the greatness of Jesus.' (Hirsch, 1842, 688). Instead it was John and Paul who initiated this alteration.

According to Hirsch, the Gospel of John turned Jesus into an abstraction rather than a historical figure; further, the Fourth Gospel ignored his Jewish background. But it is in Paul's epistles that the Church found its true roots. In the first eleven chapters of the Epistle to the Romans, Paul formulated concepts that were to become the foundation of the Church: eventually such beliefs as original sin, divine grace, and the divinity of Jesus came to separate the two faiths and were responsible for Christianity's polemic against Judaism. In explaining Paul's influence, Hirsch stressed that Paul had failed to understand the true essence of Judaism since he was attacking something he did not understand: his erroneous evaluation of the law and other doctrines were based on a misapprehension of the tradition.

> Paul carried on a sharp and violent polemic against Judaism ...unfortunately the Judaism he attacked was and is only the Judaism of Paul and his followers; it is not the Judaism of the Jews.
>
> (Hirsch, 1842, 726)

According to Hirsch, Paul's distorted views laid the foundation for the evolution of later Christian doctrine.

Although Hirsch found little of merit in Pauline Christianity, he believed that Christian faith has played a central role in history by bringing ethical monotheism to the pagan world:

> The heathens shall arrive at these thoughts, and for this reason the Pauline form of Christianity was a necessity...Therefore, the two supporting pillars (Original Sin and divine Grace) were necessary in order to bring the consciousness of the truth to the pagan world; that is the mission of the Catholic Church.
>
> (Hirsch, 1854, 243)

When paganism has been conquered, he continued, a religion of tolerance and love will be established – this, he believed, will be a purified Judaism as represented by Jesus himself. In this messianic project, Christianity has an instrumental role, but for Hirsch it is Judaism which is the only possible hope for the religious future of humanity.

SOLOMON FORMSTECHER

Like Hirsch, Solomon Formstecher – a German reform rabbi – was anxious to defend Judaism from the challenge of Christianity. In

1841 he published *The Religion of the Spirit*; in this study (which was influenced by the writings of the philosopher Friedrich Wilhelm Joseph von Schelling) Formstecher argued that ultimate reality is the Divine World Soul, a cosmic unity manifesting itself both in nature and in spirit. According to Formstecher, nature is an organic hierarchy of events and forces that attains self-consciousness in Spirit. As knowledge of nature, Spirit takes the form of logic; as knowledge of the ideal to be realized by natural objects, Spirit takes the form of aesthetics. It is thus through physics, logic and aesthetics that Spirit can become active in nature and achieve awareness of human existence through ethical ideals. As the highest form of consciousness, human beings are able to apprehend the Divine World in these manifestations of Spirit. Yet Formstecher stated that such knowledge is only symbolic – it does not depict God nor describe his essence. For Formstecher the Divine World Soul in itself remains a mystery.

In this presentation Formstecher drew a distinction between two types of religion; the religion of nature and the religion of Spirit. The religion of nature, he argued, consists of various pagan cults which defy natural forces. Paganism, he continued, culminates in 'physical monotheism' in which nature is viewed as a single divine being. Physical monotheism is thus a pantheistic conception of the world and all that is in it; within such a religious system the goal of human beings is to return to their origin in God. The religion of the Spirit however identifies God with both nature and the ethical ideal, thereby evaluating the human person above nature. In such a religious framework humans are encouraged to become like God choosing the moral good.

For Formstecher Judaism was the first religion of the Spirit, yet even within the Jewish faith there has been an evolution of ideas. Since its development takes place within the context of a religion of the Spirit, it continually remains opposed to pagan religions in the quest for perfection. 'Judaism,' he wrote, attains the stage of perfection only when its ideal is realized in the life of the individual.' (Formstecher, 1841, 70) Pagan religions on the other hand develop within the limits of their attachment to the objects of nature. Within history these two forms of religion are in constant opposition:

Paganism and Judaism must continue throughout history to develop as opponents, and they must move on until each religion has recognized and attained the ideal set for it: when paganism has reached the culmination of its development, it will be convinced that in deifying the forces of nature it has only grasped one manifestation of God. (Formstecher, 1841, 71f)

According to Formstecher, Judaism is the ultimate form of the religious life. In time all peoples will come to realize this truth, and in this unfolding of true consciousness Christianity and Islam play a crucial role:

> Christianity and Islam are the northern and southern missions of Judaism to the pagan world; they are the means used by Providence to overthrow the deification of nature and to lead the generations of man to the apex of perfection. Both are an amalgamation of Judaism with paganism, and both consider themselves to possess the absolute truth and find their mission in the task of advancing this truth till it is the common property of all mankind.
>
> (Formstecher, 1841, 411)

In Formstecher's view, Judaism cannot grant equality with these other monotheistic faiths since they embody only a few of the truths of Judaism as a means of preparing humanity for the full realization of God's providential plan: 'In essence their mission is a movement of Judaism, which leads itself through paganism and then back to itself.' (Formstecher, 1841, 365f).

For Formstecher Judaism is at the apex of the religious life. In its early stages, the Jewish faith influenced the pagan world indirectly through Christianity and Islam. As far as Christianity is concerned, its missionary role was transitory: 'Christianity recognizes salvation as its task and atonement as the goal for which it aspires....The living symbol of this salvation and atonement is found by Christianity in the death of Jesus'. (Formstecher, 1841, 369f). Despite this positive evaluation, Formstecher was critical of Christianity. In the elaboration of its ethical doctrines, the Christian faith surrounded the ethics of Judaism with the metaphysics of paganism; in addition it stripped away the ceremonies and practices peculiar to Israel, and replaced them with universalistic principles.

It is precisely these pagan elements of Christianity which constitute its central weakness. According to Formstecher,

Christianity was initially forced to adopt pagan beliefs and observances. Yet, Formstecher noted, when the Church attained power it strove to eliminate these pagan influences, however this struggle was extremely difficult because paganism had become an important feature of the Christian heritage:

> The heathen-Jewish element, which was tolerated in Judaism and which was always considered of secondary importance, became the living substratum of Christianity; it appeared as the primary Christian element, first with predominantly Jewish and then with predominantly pagan characteristics; finally it will lead back to the realm of Judaism.
>
> (Formstecher 1841, 389f)

In discussing the inherent paganism in Christianity, Formstecher pointed to a number of doctrines which, he believed, were essentially pagan in character: transubstantiation, the cult of relics, prayer for the dead, and the elevation to sainthood.

Here then in Formstecher's writing is a blend of Jewish Exclusivism and Inclusivism. In Formstecher's view, the monotheistic religions have had important roles in the unfolding of God's eschatological plan for all people – in this providential scheme both Christianity and Islam play significant – although subservient – roles in combatting paganism. In all its forms paganism is misguided and pernicious and must be defeated by these three religious traditions. Judaism however is the superior religion and the ultimate fulfilment of God's revelation to humanity. Thus Formstecher's vision of Judaism as the universal ethical religion of Spirit is Exclusivist in its rejection of paganism, but Inclusivist in its endorsement of both the Christian and Muslim Faiths.

SOLOMON LUDWIG STEINHEIM

In *According to the Doctrine of the Synagogue*, the German theologian Solomon Ludwig Steinheim maintained that Judaism should not be confused with philosophical speculation. In this work he criticized Hirsch and Formstecher for their reliance on Schelling and Hegel, and also rebuked Moses Mendelssohn for his contention that natural religion is the source of theoretical truth and that revelation consists of a code of law. According to Steinheim, the knowledge human beings acquire from the Bible consists of beliefs rather than legislation. Influenced by Kant's view that reason is unable to comprehend things-in-themselves, Steinheim argued that reason is incapable of constructing reality as perceived through ordinary experience as well as scientific investigation on *a priori* grounds. Ordinary perception and natural science, he believed, provide empirical knowledge that cannot be derived from thought; revelation however is the source of supra-rational insights that can be validated by the awareness that one is a free moral agent. Thus the content of revelation is not derived from reason, but can subsequently be verified by it.

Following Maimonides, Steinheim insisted that the central issue of theology is whether God is a free creative being. Here Steinheim distinguished between natural and revealed religion. Natural religion, he asserted, is based on the assumption that all things are caused and that nothing can come from nothing. These two concepts however are incompatible: if everything has a cause, then matter must have a cause – in consequence something can come from nothing and creation is possible. On the other hand, if nothing can come from nothing, there is no need to explain the existence of material reality – on such an account there is no need for God as First Cause. For Steinheim the only way out of this dilemma is to appeal to the revealed biblical doctrine of *creatio ex nihilo*. Hence only revealed religion, he believed, could provide a basis for the freedom which is attested by human ethical consciousness. Turning to Christianity, Steinheim argued that the Christian faith was in danger of degenerating into paganism:

> Let all those who have counterfeited our pure concept of revelation, and have adulterated it with pagan philosophical elements, rebuke as an enemy of Christianity the individual who has accused them of neglect of duty and unfaithfulness in the stewardship of their precious talent. This will not cause him to shrink back; he will rather accept this title if they speak of their own mixture as a kind of Christianity...A Christianity which is not as much based upon revelation pure and simple as upon myth and philosophy is not worthy of the name!...Let it not be called revelation and the teaching of Christ, but the very opposite, apostasy from it. It leads to the gods of Meru and Mount Olympus but not to God, who revealed Himself to Moses

upon Sinai, the God who instructed Christ and the Apostle to the Gentiles.

(Steinheim, 1863, vol. 2, xiif)

In making this claim, Steinheim sought to illustrate how pagan elements had penetrated Christianity. True revelation, he argued, is always an auditory experience whereas false revelations are visible. For Steinheim Jesus stood completely within the sphere of true revelation, but paganism had been introduced into the faith by John with his doctrine of the Trinity. As Christianity spread to other lands, such pagan features gained wide acceptance and through the ages Christian theologians have been more interested in such features of Christianity than the teaching and ministry of Jesus. In this way, the Christianity heritage has degenerated from its original Jewish purity. This, Steinheim declared, is a tragedy since the core of the Christian tradition is of religious significance. In the life of Jesus, the Jew can recognize God's providence at work:

> We have guarded ourselves categorically against the charge or the suspicion of harbouring hostile feelings against the sublime founder of the new brotherhood, the man who unlocked the sanctuary for the pagans. However we distinguish sharply...we are completely and sincerely convinced of its providential character and value as a means of attracting and overcoming paganism and dogmatic rationalism in all its forms.
>
> (Steinheim, 1863, 76f)

According to Steinheim, in ancient times the mission of the Jews was to combat natural religion; in the modern world the Jewish faith must avoid succumbing to the fashions of philosophical rationalism. In Steinheim's opinion Christianity is a combination of biblical truth and pagan ideas.

According to Steinheim the history of Christianity is an extended struggle with paganism continually victorious. At times the pagan elements of the faith have virtually destroyed its authentic religious core – it was only because of the Reformation that human progress has become possible. This was however not Luther's primary intention in his quest to reform the Church, and Steinheim offered a critical analysis of Luther's biblical exegesis as well as an attack on Luther for unleashing a wave of anti-Semitism which has continued through to the present. Nonetheless, Steinheim considered Luther's writing to be of vital importance in the Church's evolution. 'Blessed be the memory of Luther,' he wrote, 'despite every way in which he may have erred in word and deed! His memory shall also be holy for us.' (Steinheim, 1863, 246). The Reformation, Steinheim continued, was an important step on the way to human development: it has given people freedom. Yet it has not done much for revelation itself despite its contributions:

> In the midst of the circle of idolatry, which matches that of paganism in extent and intensity, amidst all the helpers, intercessors and representatives of the miserable outcast, there suddenly arose a spark which had been excluded by the Reformation.
>
> (Steinheim, 1863, 244)

For Steinheim, then, the Reformation has moved too slowly, failing to bring about the religious advances he favoured.

Unlike other thinkers of the Enlightenment Steinheim did not share the same optimism about modern thought, viewing natural science and contemporary philosophical reflection as a return to paganism. In this light he criticized Jewish emancipationists such as Mendelssohn as well as contemporary philosophers including Schelling and Hegel. Although his opinions represented a minority position, he was not deterred:

> What leads us into the struggle with these powers? – us who are weak into battle with men, into the struggle of the spirits. Let me be permitted to respond to this question with a thought of the great reformer [Luther]: 'Only when the day of universal redemption is at hand would it dawn on me to see whether I could possibly reinstate Moses again and to lead the little brooks to the right spring and river.
>
> (Steinheim, 1863, 335f)

Thus in his writing Steinheim viewed Jesus' ministry as part of God's revelation to humanity, condemning Christianity for adulterating its saviour's message and thereby descending into paganism: Christians, he believed, must engage in a struggle to reform their heritage. Jews, on the other hand, have a duty to refute natural religion and all its manifestations: as the superior faith this, he believed, should be Judaism's task in contemporary society.

HERMANN COHEN

As Jews entered the mainstream of European life, they were forced to grapple with modern currents of philosophical thought. Pre-eminent among nineteenth-century Jewish thinkers Hermann Cohen initially received a traditional Jewish education, but later became a leader of the Neo-Kantian movement and was appointed professor at the University of Marburg. Cohen's approach to Christianity was less exegetical than previous Jewish scholars; rather than concentrating on the historical background of the gospels, Cohen was concerned with Christian theology.

According to Cohen the concept of the Trinity is a pantheistic doctrine which was formulated in order to bring human beings closer to God. Yet this belief fails to accomplish this aim since Christianity links the Holy Spirit and God rather than God and Jesus. Cohen also argued that Christianity confuses the nature of God and man: 'Man does not remain man, and God does not remain God' (Cohen, 1924, vol. 3, 193). Further Cohen criticized the worship of saints as undermining humanity's highest ethical ideals. Through such hero-worship, the Church espoused perfection as an unattainable goal. Finally turning to Jesus, Cohen declared that the founder of the faith – as interpreted by contemporary Protestantism – is a threat to Judaism. Our moral feelings, he believed, must arouse a protest in us against the teaching of Jesus:

> As we do not recognize a God of suffering, so we may not recognize an ideal man either. For us, man must always remain erring and striving, striving for the highest, but erring according to human fate. For us, there can be no imitation of any man...As men, we are all equally children of the One God; no son of man is the son of God, in no sense no matter how idealized or symbolic.
>
> (Cohen, 1924, vol. 2, 128)

Cohen was also critical of the current interpretation of Jesus on historical grounds. In the gospels Jesus is idealized as caring and peaceful. Yet it is possible to derive an entirely different picture of him from Scripture.

For Jews, he was a threat to the tradition; even if he did not claim to be the son of God, Jesus asserted that he had a special relation-ship with God. Moreover, the Sermon on the Mount contains statements at odds with Judaism. The Jewish tradition, for example, does not encourage hatred of one's neighbours. Thus the life of Jesus cannot serve as an ideal personality for Jews. Here Cohen contrasts Jesus' words on the cross with various Jewish martyrs who went to their deaths reciting the words of the *Shema*.

Although Cohen respected Christianity for some of its religious teachings, he believed it was an error to encourage the Jewish community to venerate Jesus: 'We can and should recognize and honour without prejudice, but with esteem and reverence, the utterances which bear that name [i.e. Jesus]; however, we may not mitigate our opposition to the privileged position of this God-Man. Here the fate of our religion is at stake.' (Cohen, 1924, vol. 2, 128).

In presenting this case against Jesus, Cohen was anxious to stress that the historical picture of Jesus as presented by nineteenth-century scholars was irrelevant. Religious convictions, he argued, do not depend on historical events – they are based instead on individual conviction. In this respect Protestantism was mistaken in its quest to discover the historical Jesus:

> When Christ is honoured as an idea rather than a historical person or fact, then the best thoughts of ancient Christianity and the deepest characteristics of the Christian Middle Ages live on. Protestant dogma becomes much stronger, deeper, and purer when thus transmitted than through boasts about the reality of a historical person.
>
> (Cohen, 1924, vol. 2, 208)

For Cohen, what is of central importance for the individual believer is the Christ of faith rather than the Jesus of history. In his critique of Christianity, Cohen pointed out that there is a similarity between Jesus in the New Testament and the Logos in the writings of Philo, the first-century BC Jewish philosopher. In Cohen's opinion both concepts would have been incomprehensible to the Biblical prophets. For to Cohen, prophetic Judaism centred around the ethical ideals of the Jewish faith – it did not flow from God through a human incarnation. Instead God himself represents the highest morality: 'thus', he stated, 'the Jewish idea of God exhausts itself in the ethical meaning of the idea God.' (Cohen, 1924, vol. 3, 135). Christianity on the other hand is fatally flawed because the God of Christianity is no longer such an ideal; instead the concept of God in Christianity embraces the human.

Another important contrast with Judaism is Christianity's concentration on suffering. In the Jewish faith, Cohen argued, suffering is never an end in itself; yet because Christianity incorporated various pagan elements, it could portray God himself as afflicted by human suffering. In Cohen's view such an idea is abhorrent.

> In monotheism suffering is only a link in the chain of salvation; it may not become the final link. It is just a first step on the path of salvation, to the perfection of mankind in accordance with the attained perfection of the idea of the unique God.
>
> (Cohen, 1911, 275)

For Cohen, Christianity's belief in Jesus as a surrogate of humanity's suffering, guilt and punishment is a grave misconception. In this connection Cohen also criticized Christianity's emphasis on the sacrifice of Jesus. In ancient times the prophets regarded sacrifices as fundamentally related to idolatry. In time the sacrificial cult was abandoned in the course of religious progress. Unfortunately however Christianity has retained it through the symbolism of Jesus' sacrificial death. In Cohen's view this practice borders on the idolatrous.

Continuing the discussion of Christianity's divergence from Judaism, Cohen believed that Paul had misunderstood the Law and that this error has been perpetuated throughout the history of the Church. For Jewry the Law constitutes 'a protective wall against the levelling down of pure monotheism, its teachings of the reconciliation of man with God, and the salvation of man by God'. (Cohen, 1911, 181). Once Christianity had eliminated the Law as a central feature of the faith, it lost a central dimension of its Judaic inheritance.

Despite these criticisms, Cohen recognized Christianity's influence on the Jewish faith. This is evident in translations of the Hebrew Scriptures which unconsciously contain various Christian influences. It is also inherent in the way in which the Christian heritage-based on the Jewish tradition – has continued to animate Jewish consciousness:

> Much of what we, as modern men, recognize as alive in our Judaism is Christian illumination which arose out of those old, eternal foundations. Would our current notion of the Messianic

idea have been possible without the liberation of the German spirit set in motion by Martin Luther? Or would the development of medieval Jewish philosophy, which was responsible for the intensification of religious life and for its philosophical freedom, be responsible for Mendelssohn? Could Mendelssohn's Phaedon or his Jerusalem be derived historically or intellectually from Maimonides?

(Cohen, 1924, vol. 2, 93)

Christianity then inevitably exerted an influence on Judaism through the centuries, and in his vision of the future, Cohen envisaged Protestantism coming even closer to its Jewish roots. This rapprochement has been prepared by the emergence of biblical criticism which has called into question the Church's reliance on traditional dogma:

Modern piety, particularly in Germany, no longer depends on the text of the dogma, but sees the kernel of belief and seeks its truth in the distinctive elements of religious ethics for men as individuals and for all the nations of the world. The ethical elements of revelation are emphasized and honoured rather than philosophizing on the existence of God.

(Cohen, 1924, vol. 2, 305f)

Such an affinity between Protestantism and Judaism however does not mean that the distinction between these two traditions will disappear. On the contrary, Protestant Christianity will continue to remain a separate faith. Nonetheless Cohen felt that Jews should encourage Protestants to promote the highest ideals. 'We neither await or promote the abolition or dissolution of Christianity,' he wrote, 'rather we wish and shall encourage all those profound endeavours which exert themselves to its idealization' (Cohen, 1924, 1:64). In considering the future, Cohen pleaded for a better relationship between the two faiths – in return he expected Christians to respect Judaism. Such mutual tolerance, he believed, would result in the creation of a better world in which monotheism would be accepted by all. According to Cohen, in accomplishing this divinely appointed role of bringing knowledge of the one true God to all nations, the Jewish people can be aided by the purer forms of the Christian faith.

CLAUDE MONTEFIORE

A more sympathetic view of Christianity was espoused by the British writer Claude G. Montefiore. In contrast to other scholars, he did not seek to demonstrate Judaism's superiority to the Christian faith. Influenced by biblical criticism, Hegelian thought, and the theory of evolution, Montefiore believed in progressive revelation and the eventual enlightenment of humanity. In this light he viewed the New Testament from a Jewish perspective, discussed the founders of the Christian faith, and sought to introduce Christianity to the Jewish community. Nonetheless he was aware that such investigations would in all likelihood evoke suspicion and hostility from his co-religionists:

> The teaching of Jesus has not been much discussed and appraised as a whole. And where it has been so discussed, the line has been rather to depreciate or to cheapen. Jewish writers have looked for parallels or for defects. Considering what Judaism and Jews have had to suffer at Christian hands, this Jewish treatment of the Gospels is not astonishing.
>
> (Montefiore, 1927, xxi)

In spite of such a negative response, Montefiore was committed to reappraising Christianity. This task, he believed, would fall primarily to Liberal Jews. 'Liberal Judaism,' he wrote, 'does not believe that God has enabled the human race to reach forward to religious truth so exclusively through a single channel.' (Montefiore, 1918, 78). As a result, other religions need to be studied so as to gain knowledge of God's disclosure: because Montefiore felt most capable of exploring Christianity, he was committed to this enterprise.

According to Montefiore, Liberal Jews are obliged to understand and appreciate the Christian tradition as part of their religious heritage. The New Testament, he stressed, belongs to Judaism:

> It is a book which, in very large part, was written by persons who were born Jews. Its central hero was a Jew. Its teaching is based throughout – sometimes indeed by way of opposition – upon the teaching of the Old Testament.
>
> (Montefiore, 1918, 80)

As a result Montefiore became an apologist for the Christian faith, seeking to present the best of the tradition to a Jewish audience. Writing about the New Testament, he stated:

> The Liberal Jew at any rate will not be deterred from gaining all the good he can from the Gospels (or from the rest of the New Testament) because there are many things in it which he holds to be erroneous. It also contains a lower and a higher. So too the Prophets, but he does not therefore reject them.
>
> (Montefiore, 1927, cxliii)

In his discussion of Jesus' ministry, Montefiore rejected the miraculous aspects of the New Testament account; instead he focused on the parallels between the Jewish and Christian faiths. In *Rabbinic Literature and the Gospel Teachings* as well as *The Synoptic Gospels*, he traced these connections. Given such links between the Christian writings and Judaism, Montefiore emphasized that Jews should be inspired by the teachings of Christianity:

> We have...brought together in words of striking simplicity and power in the pages of the Gospels. Shall we admire and cherish, and learn from, these exquisite stories, or shall we sniff and sneer at them and pass them by?
>
> (Montefiore, 1918, 86)

Regarding the New Testament itself, Montefiore viewed Jesus as part of the prophetic tradition. 'If Jesus resembled the prophets in the cause and occasion of his preaching,' he wrote, 'still more did he resemble them in his temper of mind, and therefore in one great feature and characteristic of his teaching....The inwardness of Jesus, the intense spirituality of his teaching, need not be insisted on here. I only emphasize it now to show his connection and kinship with the Prophets.' (Montefiore, 1910, 19). According to Montefiore, Jesus' sayings should be understood in the context of the prophetic tradition. Here Montefiore stressed that Jesus did not seek to violate Jewish law:

> It is even doubtful whether, except perhaps in cases or moments of stress and conflict, he sought or desired or intended to put his

own teaching in direct contrast with, or substitution for, the
teaching of those around him, or the teaching of the Law.

> (Montefiore, 1927, 80)

Rather like the prophets, Jesus wished to affirm the importance of
the moral law:

> Jesus...had to hark back from the Law to the Prophets. His
> teaching is a revival of prophetic Judaism, and in some respects
> points forward to the Liberal Judaism of today.
>
> (Montefiore, 1927, cxxxiv)

In describing Jesus' statements, Montefiore asserted that in some
cases his sayings (such as 'Love thy enemies') were by necessity
exaggerated for emphasis. This fact he believed, has not been
appreciated by the Jewish community. In Montefiore's view Jesus'
utterances were entirely consistent with traditional Jewish
theology. For example, when Jesus spoke about the Kingdom of
God, he did not detach himself from the tradition. Further, in areas
of philosophy and theology Montefiore maintained that Jesus
added little new. It was later Christian writers who reinterpreted
and expanded his message.

What Montefiore admired most in the Gospels was Jesus'
heroism: 'That heroic element seems to show itself in a certain
grand largeness of views and in a certain grand simplicity. Taken
as a whole, this heroic element is full of genius and inspiration. We
must not always take it literally, and squeeze out of it too literal an
application. The letter of even the prophet's teachings may kill;
here too we must sometimes look only to the spirit.' (Montefiore,
1918, 103)

Avoiding the traditional Christian doctrines of the Incarnation
and the Trinity, Montefiore emphasized Jesus' nobility:

> We seem to see, through the mist of eulogy and legend, the sure
> outlines of a noble personality. Here we have a deeply religious
> nature, filled, as perhaps few before or after have been filled,
> with the love of God and the consciousness of his presence... A
> teacher stands before us who is not only a teacher, but hero,
> strong, sometimes even passionate, fervent, devoted brave....He
> is filled with a true Jewish idealism, for there is no more idealistic
> race that of Israel....He has no ambition except one; to do the will

of his Father in Heaven, and to serve the people to whom he has been sent' (Montefiore, 1918, 126f).

Despite this positive assessment of Jesus' character, Montefiore recognized inconsistencies in his teaching; these, however, were matters of minor significance. Nonetheless it was largely because of these defects that Montefiore was unable to accept the Christian understanding of Jesus. 'I would not deny that the dogma of the Incarnation of God as Jesus has had its effects for good as well as evil,' he wrote. 'But Liberal Jews do hold that it rests on a confusion, the confusion of a man with God.' (Montefiore 1927, xxv).

In assessing Paul's contribution to the development of Christianity, Montefiore attempted to explain his views in the context of first century Judaism. In contrast with other Jewish scholars, he was not disturbed by Paul's writings:

> In spite of his amazing forgetfulness of the Jewish doctrine of repentance and atonement, in spite too of the remoteness for us of his opposition 'law versus Christ', we may still admire the profundity and genius and adopt many true and noble elements of his religious and ethical teaching.
>
> (Montefiore, 1923, 174)

According to Montefiore Paul's attitude toward the Law has been widely misunderstood; the Judaism he attacked was not rabbinic Judaism. This tradition was 'poor, more pessimistic...it possessed these inferiorities just because it was not Rabbinic Judaism, but Diaspora Judaism (Montefiore, 1914, 93). The form of Judaism that Paul knew was solely that of the Diaspora, therefore it is a mistake to see him as an enemy of the rabbis. For Montefiore the greatness of Paul is attested by the autobiographical passages of the epistles: 'There is always something inspiring in the picture of a great man, convinced of his cause, and pursuing his straight course in the face of constant opposition and trial. Paul not only rises superior to his sufferings, but he exults and rejoices in them.' (Montefiore, 1914, 179).

In his writings then Montefiore wished to present Christianity in the most positive light. In his view the New Testament contains religious truths which are of vital importance for the Jewish community. In Jesus, he believed, Jewry can recognize a prophetic figure of great proportions, similarly Paul stands out as a spiritual figure of significance. Committed to the belief in the progressive revelation of God's will, he was convinced that God was at work in the lives of these two founders of the Christian faith. Because of his personal interests, he confined his discussion to the Judeo-Christian tradition, yet he was convinced that God had revealed himself within other religious traditions as well. In this respect we can see in his writings the outlines of a theory of Jewish Pluralism consonant with the presupposition of Liberal Judaism.

7

Modern Jewish Thought

In the modern period a number of Jewish theologians have been anxious to explore the origins of Christianity, its subsequent development, and the relationship between the Jewish and Christian faiths. The Central European writer, Max Brod, for example, admired Jesus as a Jewish teacher. Yet he was critical of Paul's view that God's revelation was manifest in a single historical event – the life of Christ; in addition, he argued that as the Christian faith developed it became corrupted by pagan features. In his opinion the only hope for the human race is Judaism. The German Jewish theologian Franz Rosenzweig was not concerned with the life of Jesus; rather he was preoccupied with theological truth. According to Rosenzweig, paganism does not offer a viable approach to God; Judaism and Christianity on the other hand provide a true path to the Divine. Judaism, he believed, expresses the relationship between God, humanity and the world – nonetheless Christianity has the capacity to spread the universal message of monotheism to all peoples. A positive endorsement of the Christian faith was similarly affirmed by the German Jewish leader Leo Baeck who attempted to reclaim Jesus as an authentic Jewish figure despite Baeck's criticism of Pauline Christianity and the subsequent development of Christian theology. Likewise the German Jewish theologian Martin Buber admired Jesus as a great religious figure despite his misguided messianic claims. Even though Jews cannot accept Jesus as Saviour, he argued, they should recognize his essential Jewishness. A similar plea was expressed by Jacob Klausner, formerly professor at the Hebrew University. Jesus, he maintained, was a typical Jewish teacher of the first century who fully accepted Jewish law; as such he should be regarded with respect by the Jewish community. In Klausner's view, Judaism will eventually become the religion for all people – nevertheless Jews should acknowledge their debt to Christianity for paving the way for this outcome.

MAX BROD

Among the leading Jewish thinkers of Central Europe, Max Brod
was of central importance in addressing the issue of religious
pluralism. Born in Prague, he became a Zionist while at the same
time advocating universalistic ideas. In *Heidentum, Christentum,
Judentum*, he discussed the attitudes of pagans, Christians and Jews
to the world and the Hereafter. Eschewing historical analysis, Brod
began by considering the approach of these religious paths to evil
or misfortunes. Evil, he argued, can be divided into two aspects:
noble and ignoble misfortune. Noble misfortune consists of
humanity's basic imperfections – these are part of the human
condition, and it is fruitless to struggle against these features of the
human personality. Ignoble misfortune, on the other hand, denotes
those imperfections which can be overcome (such as social and
economic deprivation). Some of these defects are due to human
motivation; others, such as disease, are related to the battle for
survival.

In espousing this view, Brod was preoccupied with the gulf
between the human and the divine. Every person, he asserted, is
driven to establish a relationship with God which will help him in
the battle with ignoble misfortune. Various responses to this issue
are offered by paganism, Christianity and Judaism. In Brod's
opinion, one of these religious paths is destined to predominate in
the future:

> All depends upon whether paganism, Christianity, or Judaism
> will rise to become the future ideal of the world.
>
> (Brod, 1922, vol. 1, 9)

According to Brod, paganism's affirmation of the world has been
transmuted into contemporary Marxism and other leftist doctrines.
Christianity however lacks such an optimistic standpoint – for the
Christian human life is overwhelmed by Original Sin, and the
world requires divine intervention for redemption to take place.
For this reason many people have abandoned religion for secular
ideologies based on human endeavour. Judaism on the contrary
acknowledges human imperfection, but maintains that the world
can be perfected through messianic activity. Salvation is thus not
relegated to the Hereafter, but is confined to the here and now.
According to Brod this makes Judaism the ideal solution to

problems facing contemporary society. 'According to the pagan concept,' he wrote, 'it (the divine) is used to strengthen the orderly progress within this world...according to the Christian view (the divine) manages to break the limits of this world due to the pressure of its metaphysical power...according to Jewish feeling both this world and the tasks of the world...suddenly appear new to the man filled with the spirit of God...henceforth they will be able to continue beside and through God. It will be possible in the here and now to combat the ignoble misfortune without endangering eternal salvation.' (Brod, 1922, 228)

In distinguishing between these three religious paths, Brod was critical of the way in which Christianity had misconstrued Jesus' ministry. In Brod's view Christianity used Jesus in its denial of ignoble misfortune. The Christian faith, he wrote, sees God's revelation in a single moment of history rather than, as in Judaism, in continuous intervention. For the Christian all experience is determined by the incarnation of God in Christ: 'The Christian possesses his prescribed route; he awaits the appearance of God from one particular direction in a particular form – in Christian belief.' (Brod, 1952, 458ff). This is the ultimate disclosure, and the Christian need only encounter Christ for his salvation. Brod believed that such an outlook is far too narrow, restraining human beings from engaging in building God's kingdom on earth.

In this discussion, Brod distinguished between Protestantism and Catholicism: 'Protestantism presents itself as the logical structured system of Christianity; indeed, therefore, it collides even more violently with the ethical realities of the world and of the heart of man. It is simply unwilling to allow itself to be debased. In contrast, Catholicism is a more elastic machine of divine grace. It would allow reality its place and would fit itself to the truth, however, without abandoning the false premises of the prescribed route of its march to divine grace.' (Brod, 1952, vol. 2, 88f)

Despite this distinction, Brod believed that human freedom is eliminated by both forms of Christianity – if Jesus died for the sins of the world, nothing is left for individual action. Only Judaism awaits the salvation of God which is not found in a single cosmic moment, but in human potential and action. 'Freedom of the will,' he wrote, 'can...exist besides "grace", but only when enunciated in the Jewish manner, as grace derived directly from God. It is not possible alongside grace comprehended in the Christian manner.' (Brod, 1952, vol. 2, 102).

In his exposition of the weaknesses of the Christian faith, Brod focused on the figure of Paul. According to Brod, Christianity's dogmatic belief in Jesus was a development of Pauline thought:

> Paul believed in the redeeming Christ, for himself. That, however, was his personal salvation, his individual path to salvation and so religiously appropriate. He generalized this path and that was religiously wrong.
>
> (Buber, 1948, 160f)

Thus according to Brod, Paul's views were authentically Jewish when applied to himself, but the universalization of his thought went beyond the realm of the Jewish tradition. For Paul Jesus was not simply an exemplary person whom he wished to emulate – he was the Christ who had died for all. This meant that the Jewish concept of salvation was narrowed to the sacrificial death of Jesus – Paul's own mystical experience was thus to become a paradigm for all humanity. Such a notion however was a distortion of Jesus' life and death.

Despite this criticism, Brod admired Paul as a noble Jewish type. Judaism, he explained, continually produced such individuals rather than the brutal heroes of other nations. The Jews, he wrote, 'produce the type of active martyrs, martyrs of their cause rather than martyrs who are an end in themselves or whose martyrdom is the crown of their life; for them it is incidental.' (Buber, 1948, 176f). Even though Paul had misconstrued the meaning of Jesus' life and death, Brod believed that the Jewish community should not overlook Paul's greatness: 'Although Judaism remains incalculably rich in its humane heroes, it can never be so rich as not to miss a figure like Paul in its midst. It would be parochial and petty to exclude him because of the consequences his actions unwittingly brought forth.' (Buber, 1948, 176f).

Continuing his discussion of Christian origins and historical development, Brod criticized modern Christianity as an amalgamation of the traditional Christian faith and paganism. Up to the sixteenth century, he stated, Christianity struggled against paganism. Since then however, pagan elements have penetrated the tradition:

> This Christian-pagan cultural amalgam, which in time sequence is the last link in the development of Christianity, absolutely

rules the present day world. It has formed and conquered this period as no other pattern of thought before.

(Buber, 1948, 235)

In launching this attack, Brod asserted that contemporary Christianity appears to favour love, nobility and other virtues, but in fact it remains indifferent to everything of this world; as a consequence it has not been difficult to misuse the Christian faith in support of politics and modern warfare.

For Brod then Christianity has made an important contribution to humanity yet its failures outweigh its benefits. Although he admired both Jesus and Paul, Brod believed that the Christian faith – under Paul's influence – had been mistaken in assuming that God's revelation was manifest in a single historical event: the life of Christ. Such an approach, Brod believed, was too narrow and stifled human enterprise. In addition, as the Christian faith developed over the centuries, it absorbed pagan features and thereby became corrupted. In his view the only religious hope for humanity is Judaism which has remained true to its most lofty ideals.

FRANZ ROSENZWEIG

Among modern thinkers the German Jewish philosopher Franz Rosenzweig occupies a central role. In common with Hermann Cohen, Rosenzweig was not interested in the historicity of Jesus; rather he was preoccupied with theological truth. Such a concern was generated by the fact that several of his friends including Eugen Rosenstock-Huessy and Rudolf Ehrenburg became Christians and attempted to persuade him to make the same decision.

Rosenzweig believed that as a Jew, he could view Christianity impartially; Christians however could not be equally objective about Judaism because of their missionary intent. Nonetheless, Rosenzweig felt that the modern period offered new opportunities for both religious communities to reach a greater degree of understanding. Given this situation, he sought to explain the nature of the Jewish faith to his recently converted friends. Yet he recognized that this would not be an easy task:

I realize that everything I wrote is beyond my power to express to you. For I should now need to show you Judaism from within...just as you would have to show Christianity to me, an outsider. Just as you cannot do this, neither can I. The soul of Christianity lies in its expressions; while Judaism shows only its hard, protective shell to the outer world; only within can one speak of its soul.

(Rosenzweig, 1935, 688)

Despite such obstacles, Rosenzweig was anxious to compare both traditions. These faiths, he argued, have a special status granted to no other religion. Paganism, he believed, contains no valid approach to the Divine; Judaism and Christianity, on the other hand, share God, revelation, prayer, and final redemption. These eternal verities constitute their common ground. Rosenzweig represented this shared basis symbolically with Israel as the star and Christianity as the rays:

The truth, the entire truth, belongs neither to them nor to us. We bear it within ourselves, precisely, therefore, we must first gaze within ourselves, if we wish to see it. So we will see the star, but not its rays. To encompass the whole truth one must not only see the light but also what it illumines. They, on the other hand, have been eternally destined to see the illuminated object, but not the light.

(Rosenzweig, 1930, vol. 3, 200f)

On this view truth appears only in a divided form: the Jewish way and the Christian way. However before God it is united. For Rosenzweig, the roles of Judaism and Christianity are symbolized by the image of a star burning at its core and sending out rays. Judaism's self-absorption is represented by the burning core whereas Christianity's worldliness is symbolized by the rays sent forth from the star's centre: 'The rays go forth only from the fire,' he wrote, 'and flow unresisted to the outside. The fire of the core must burn incessantly. Its flame must eternally feed upon itself. It requires no fuel without.'

(Rosenzweig, 1970, 298)

Following this image, the burning star does not require its rays – it continues to burn even if the rays are blocked in the process of radiation. The rays on the other hand require the continuous burning of the star's core. Christianity is thus dependent on

Judaism, but not vice versa. On this view Christianity has not overcome the Jewish tradition; rather Judaism must continue to nurture Christian faith.

This astronomical image was used by Rosenzweig to highlight the different roles of these two faiths in God's eternal plan. Creation, Rosenzweig believed, is constituted as God's relationship with the world; revelation, as God's relationship with man; and redemption as the final reconciliation between God-related human beings and a God-related world. This final stage will result in the direct relationship of everything with God. In this process Jews and Christians hold fast to their different traditions. Judaism, he believed, constitutes the basic relationship between God, humanity, and the world. Christianity on the other hand has the unique function to include all nations in the revealed relationship with God. Because of its own particularistic nature, Judaism cannot perform this redemptive function – if it were to do so, it would lose the unique intensity of its relationship with God. Thus Jewry must recognize the indispensable universalistic ministry of Christianity for the sake of the final redemption.

According to Rosenzweig Jewish identity is dependent on birth and brings with it covenantal obligation; the Christian however is not a Christian by birth, but only by accepting correct beliefs. Such personal commitment is necessary for the Jews. 'We possess what the Christian will one day experience,' he wrote, 'we have it from the time of our birth and through our birth it is in our blood. The antecedent of the experience goes back beyond our birth to the antiquity of our people.' (Rosenzweig, 1935, 356). Because Jews are born into this special relationship with God, Rosenzweig believed that it is impossible for a Jew to convert to Christianity. Such a state of affairs has crucial implications for Jewry in their relationship to Christianity as well as other faiths:

The Christian is by nature, or at least by birth, a heathen, while the Jew is a Jew. So the path of the Christian must consist of discarding of his self; he must constantly leave his self and oppose his self in order to become a Christian. By contrast, the life of the Jew does not lead him from his self; he must strive to live more fully within himself. The more he finds himself, the more he abandons paganism, which lies outside of him, not within himself as with the Christian.

(Rosenzweig, 1930, vol. 3, 190f)

Despite his positive evaluation of Christianity, Rosenzweig (like other Jewish thinkers) was critical of Incarnational theology. The Christian way into the land of God, he explained, is divided into two paths – a dualism which is plainly incomprehensible to the Jew, but nevertheless forms the foundation of Christian life. The Christian, he contrasted, has no hesitation in approaching the Son with the sort of reverence Jews display toward the Father: 'Only by holding the hand of the Son, does the Christian dare to approach the Father; he believes that he may only come to the Father through the Son. If the Son had not been a man, then he would be useless to the Christian. He cannot conceive that God Himself, the only God, could descend far enough for his needs.' (Rosenzweig, 1930, vol. 3, 114f).

According to Rosenzweig, such conceptions are unacceptable. In the end of days the Christian will come to see that such notions will no longer hold sway, and all peoples will acknowledge the Jewish conception of God. At the end of history there will be a universal recognition that the Jewish God is the Lord of all creation. Then no one will approach the Father except through him. This is currently the situation of the Jewish people, but in time it will become a universal truth. Thus despite Rosenzweig's statement that 'the entire truth belongs neither to them nor to us', Rosenzweig endorsed the classic Jewish view that Judaism will be the final form of the religion of humanity. Inherent then in Rosenzweig's presentation of Judaism and Christianity was the presupposition that the Christian faith would ultimately lead to a universal Judaism. Such a modernist form of Jewish Inclusivism provided a framework for a sympathetic understanding and appreciation of Christianity's role in the unfolding of God's plan for humanity – yet in the end Rosenzweig held firm to the conviction that Judaism is the only hope for the world.

LEO BAECK

Until his deportation to Theresienstadt in 1943, the liberal theologian Leo Baeck exerted a profound influence on German Jewish thought. In 1900 the Christian theologian Adolf Harnack published *The Essence of Christianity*, a liberal interpretation of Jesus and a humanistic account of early Christianity. Baeck criticized this work for ignoring rabbinic literature in its evaluation of first century

Christianity. Several years later Baeck himself published an apologetic work, *The Essence of Judaism*, which was in part an attack on Harnack's book; in this study Baeck offered a modern evaluation of Judaism. Subsequently he published other works dealing with various aspects of the Christian faith.

In many of his essays, Baeck sought to illuminate the Jewish background to the New Testament as well as chart a path of reconciliation. This, he believed, was of vital importance since for nineteen centuries Jews and Christians had regarded one another with suspicion and hostility:

> The usual, and inevitable, result of any talk was an increase in the feeling, on the Christian side, of being uncompromisingly rejected by the Jew, and on the Jewish side, of being forcibly summoned and violently accused by the Christian – let alone the fact of the restrictions and burdens imposed on the Jew, or on behalf of, the Church.
>
> (Baeck, 1954, 102f)

In contemporary society however new opportunities for dialogue have arisen, and Baeck stressed that it is imperative that both communities take advantage of these changed circumstances. Unlike previous occasions – particularly in the Middle Ages – when Jews and Christians engaged in disputation, such encounters should be conducted with respect and tolerance.

In exploring the nature of Judaism, Baeck drew attention to various features which distinguished it from Christianity. Explaining why the Jewish faith does not need the kind of dogmatic formulation of belief as in Christianity, he wrote:

> In it [Judaism] there was no need for a constant, inviolable formula; this is necessary only in those religions at the heart of which lies a mystical consecrating faith – an act which alone can open the door to salvation and which therefore requires a definite conceptual image to be handed down from age to age. Such acts of salvation and gifts of grace are alien to Judaism; it does not pretend to be able to bring heaven to earth. It has always maintained a certain sobriety and severity, demanding even more than it gives. This is why it adopted so many commandments, and refused sacraments and mysteries.
>
> (Baeck, 1948, 13)

Continuing this theme Baeck argued that the romantic feature inherent in Christianity originated with Paul who infused Oriental mystery cults into nascent Christianity. As this new religion developed, it became passive in character. According to Baeck, such an orientation had a significant impact on Western culture – it led to the notion of the 'finished man', an individual who believes he possesses absolute truth: 'Since the end of the ancient world,' he wrote, 'the intellectual life of the Occident has in many ways been determined by this notion. It has established that orientation in which the answer precedes every question.' (Baeck, 1958, 206). In the Middle Ages, such a conviction dominated the age and was hardly affected by the Reformation. It was only with the French Revolution and the Enlightenment that free thought has been able to prevail. However in contrast with 'romantic religion', 'classical religion' – as represented by Judaism – embodies a hopeful optimism and respect for human freedom.

In his writing Baeck was also concerned with Christian origins. In *The Gospel as a Document of the History of the Jewish Faith*, he examined the Jewish background of the Gospels. In this work he sought to strip the Gospels of later accretions in order to reconstruct the original documents. According to Baeck, the Gospels were derived from oral traditions that were later written down; those who wrote the gospels, he argued, were like the Jewish sages who recorded the Jewish oral tradition:

> These men, too, experienced everything in terms of the Bible, and the words of Scripture directed, commanded, and exerted an inner compulsion. For these men, too, a fixed content, a fixed religious doctrine, was there to begin with and was most vividly real and the whole truth. For them, too, and for those who received the tradition from them, their master's lot and fate had long been revealed and always preordained...The tradition of the Gospel is, first of all, in every one of these respects, simply a part of the Jewish tradition of that time.
>
> (Baeck, 1958, 63)

Later however the thought pattern of the Hellenistic world influenced the initial Christian vision and led to fundamental changes in the transmission of the Gospel. Yet it was possible, Baeck believed, to discover Jesus' original teaching: 'On the whole,' he wrote, 'it is nevertheless possible to get back to the original tradition. If one notes the special characteristics of each of the three authors and, so to say, eliminates them, the procedure and method to be followed after that can be shown quite clearly...The following, on the other hand, must be part of the old original tradition: whatever is completely different from the tendencies and purposes of the generations which came after the first generation of disciples; whatever contradicts the tenets which later became part of the faith; whatever is different from, or even opposed to, the intellectual, psychic, and political climate in which these later generations gradually found themselves; whatever, in other words, exemplifies the way of life and the social structure, the climate of thought and feeling, the way of speaking and the style of Jesus' own environment and time. In all this we are confronted with the words and deeds of Jesus.' (Baeck, 1958, 99f).

After an examination of the life of Jesus in the light of this method, Baeck concluded that Jesus was a Jewish figure firmly rooted in the tradition of his ancestors:

> In the old Gospel which is thus opened up before us, we encounter a man with noble features who lived in the land of the Jews in tense and excited times and helped and laboured and suffered and died: a man out of the Jewish people who walked on Jewish paths with Jewish faith and hopes. His spirit was at home in the Holy Scriptures, and his imagination and thought were anchored there; and he proclaimed and taught the word of God because God had given it to him to hear and to preach...In this old tradition we behold a man who is Jewish in every feature and treat of his character, manifesting in every particular what is pure and good in Judaism.
>
> (Baeck, 1958, 100f)

On this account the original Gospel was a thoroughly Jewish book firmly standing within the Jewish tradition. Baeck thus reclaimed Jesus for the Jewish people; in his view the Jesus of history was fully a Jew. The Christ of faith, on the other hand, was a deviation from history, a creation of the Greco-Roman world. Jewish history and reflection should therefore not pass Jesus by – instead he should be perceived as a Jewish personage firmly rooted in the tradition.

Turning to Paul, Baeck maintained that he was the individual responsible for this basic change in Christian thought. Profoundly influenced by Hellenism as well as the mystery religions of Asia Minor, Paul interjected foreign elements into this new Jewish movement. 'This man, Paul from Tarsus,' he wrote, 'joined the congregation of Jesus' adherents; and one day he began to preach and spread his own new faith and a new theology. What found its place here was not the doctrine of Jesus, but a doctrine about him, not his own faith which he had communicated to his disciplines but faith in him.' (Baeck, 1958, 72). Such a conception radically altered the nature of Christian belief and profoundly affected the history of the Church. As a result of Paul's teaching the theo-centric faith of Jesus was superseded by a Christ-centered faith – this change initiated a parting of the ways between Judaism and Christianity. For Baeck, subsequent Church history consisted of a struggle between the Jewish elements of the Christian faith and the Pauline features of Christianity:

> One may say that the history of the dogmas of the Church is actually a history of Judaism within the Church, that it has its various phases, according as the active ethical-psychological element of Judaism with its emphasis on the personal, or the passive magically sacramental element of faith of Paulinism, with its dissolution of that which is individual into the metaphysical is brought more strongly into prominence.
>
> (Baeck, 1925, 136)

In his treatment of Christianity then, Baeck was anxious to uncover the Jewish foundations of the Christian faith. His presentation of the Jewishness of Jesus was an attempt to reclaim Jesus as an authentic Jewish figure of the past – this way he sought to encourage the Jewish community to discover common ground with Christianity. Yet his discussion of the ways in which the original Christian message was reformulated under Paul and subsequently through Greco-Roman thought illustrates his conviction that the Church misconstrued Jesus' original message. For Baeck, Christianity as it developed through the centuries degenerated into a 'romantic religion' and in this sense has been unable to attain the spiritual purity of the 'classical religion' from which it sprang.

MARTIN BUBER

Born in Austria, the Jewish theologian Martin Buber lived in Germany and emigrated to Israel in 1933 where he taught at the Hebrew University in Jerusalem. Throughout his life he was concerned with Jewish–Christian relations, and in 1933 he engaged in one of the earliest Jewish–Christian dialogues with the German Christian theologian Karl Ludwig Schmidt. In this encounter Buber emphasized the difficulties involved in understanding the religious views of another:

> We may attempt something very difficult, something very difficult for the man with religious ties; it strains his ties and relationships or rather seems to strain ties. It seems to strain his relationship with God: We can acknowledge as a mystery that which someone else confesses as the reality of his faith, though it opposes our own existence and is contrary to the knowledge of our own being. We are not capable of judging its meaning, because we do not know it from within as we know ourselves from within.
>
> (Buber, 1936, 152)

Acknowledging that one can only approach Christianity as an outsider, Buber respected Christian religious convictions – yet he rejected the Christian claim that the world had been redeemed. Such a rejection was not based on hard-heartedness; rather it was grounded on Jewish experience:

> We understand the Christology of Christianity throughout as an important event which has taken place between the world above and the world below. We see Christianity as something...we are unable to penetrate. But just as we know that there is air which we breathe into our lungs, we also know that there is a space in which we move; more deeply, more genuinely, we know that the history of the world has not yet been shattered to its very core, that the world is not yet redeemed.
>
> (Buber, 1936, 154)

Despite such an impasse, Buber believed there can be positive discussion between Judaism and Christianity in which the participants do not reach any agreement but nevertheless respect each other for the sake of the one true God. This was Buber's point of departure and hope for the future. 'What joins Jews and Christians together,' he wrote, 'is their common knowledge about one uniqueness...Every authentic sanctuary can acknowledge the mystery of every other authentic sanctuary. The mystery of the other one is internal to the latter and cannot be perceived from without. No one outside Israel can understand the mystery of Israel. And no one outside Christendom can understand the mystery of Christendom...We should acknowledge our fundamental difference and impart to each other with unreserved confidence our knowledge of the unity of this house, a unity which we hope will one day surround us without divisions. We will serve, until the day when we may be united in common service.' (Buber, 1936, 155f).

In his writings Buber dealt with various aspects of Christianity, but the most extensive discussion of the Christian faith was presented in *Two Types of Faith*, an examination of Jesus and Paul. Like other Jewish scholars, Buber focused on the Jewish elements of Jesus' preaching; Jesus, he believed, stood firmly within the Jewish tradition:

> From my youth onwards I have found Jesus my great brother. That Christianity has regarded and does regard him as God and Saviour has always appeared to me a fact of the highest importance which, for his sake and my own, I must endeavour to understand...My own fraternally open relationship to him has grown ever stronger and clearly than ever before. I am more than ever certain that a great place belongs to him in Israel's history of faith and that this place cannot be described by any of the usual categories.
>
> (Buber, 1961, 12f)

For Buber Jesus was rooted to his Judaic past, and he compared him to numerous false Messiahs in the history of Israel:

> Jesus is the first in the series of men who acknowledged to themselves in their words their messiahship and thus stepped out of the seclusion of the servants of God, which is the real 'messianic secret'. That this First One...was incomparably the purest, most rightful of them all, the one most endowed with real

messianic power, does not alter the fact that he was the first, yet, it belongs rather to it, belongs to the awful and pathetic character of reality which clings to the whole messianic series.

(Buber, 1960, 110)

Jesus was mistaken in his messianic claims – Jews, Buber believed, must therefore reject him. Nonetheless there was nothing inherently alien to Judaism in Jesus' teaching. Following the prophetic tradition, Jesus demanded from his followers complete trust in God. Because of his close affinity to Judaism, Buber maintained that Jesus and the Pharisees were not far apart despite their divergent attitudes to the Law. In Buber's view, Jesus did not seek to abolish the commandments – he simply interpreted them in a different fashion from his opponents. In this light the Sermon on the Mount should be understood as a reformulation of basic Jewish teaching. Analyzing these words of Jesus, Buber concluded that:

The attitude of the Sermon on the Mount to the Torah appears to be the opposite of that of the Pharisees; in reality is it only a sublimation of a Pharisaic doctrine from a definite and fundamental point of view.

(Buber, 1961, 63)

Examining the statements in the Sermon on the Mount Buber argued that 'three of them (murder, adultery, oaths) derive essentially from three of the Ten Commandments and transcend them, but what they demand is to be found also in Pharisaic teachings, yet without these approaching the forcefulness of his address. The other three...refer to the commandments and precepts outside the decalogue, and either contradict them or contradict at least an accepted, apparently popular interpretation.' (Buber, 1961, 65–8). Buber was convinced that Jesus intended even these statements to fit into the tradition by subjecting the Torah to change and development. Thus the difference between Jesus and the Pharisees should be conceived as a difference in orientation:

Jesus speaks throughout as the authentic interpreter: as long as he remains standing on Sinai he teaches what the Pharisees teach, but then Sinai cannot satisfy him and he must advance into the cloud-area of the intention of the revelation.

(Buber, 1961, 65–8)

In Buber's view Jesus neither rejected Judaism nor the Covenant – the theological as opposed to the historical Jesus was the creation of later writers. 'If we consider the Synoptic and Johanine Gospels,' he wrote, 'with the disciples as two stages along one road, we immediately see what was gained and lost in the course of it. The gain was the most sublime of all theologies; it was procured at the expense of the plain concrete and situation-bound dialogicism of the original man of the Bible.' (Buber, 1961, 34). In Buber's view, Paul was the crucial figure in this development. The most important aspect of Paul's thought was his insistence on faith in Christ – this was the starting point in the doctrine of justification by faith: the simple face-to-face relationship between God and humanity was replaced by Christ's mediation. Contrary to Scripture, Paul conceived of a straight path from election to revelation to salvation. On this account, 'only God himself can effect the propitiation of an infinite guilt, by making his son, the Christ, the atoning sufferer upon himself.' (Buber, 1961, 149f).

For Buber such mediation led to a form of Christian dualism in which the world was divided into two realms: the sacred and the profane. Whatever human beings do is unholy, especially when their actions are motivated by basic human drives:

> A fundamental dualism in existence resulted: Spirit and world became subject to different laws: man can accomplish nothing by himself...All he can do is surrender to the other, to redemption which has come from beyond and has assumed bodily shape in his earthly sphere.
>
> (Buber, 1948, 178f)

Christianity had thus created a dualism in nature; such a dichotomy, Buber believed, eventually resulted in a deep-seated pessimism which he firmly rejected. Judaism, on the other hand, extolled all of creation and stressed the importance of human endeavour. Following this theme, Buber criticized those periods of Christian history which were dominated by Pauline thought. In the modern world, Buber argued, the Pauline conception of faith should be replaced by the Jewish emphasis on human activity and enterprise.

In his writing, then, Buber expressed admiration for Jesus; Jews, he maintained, should attempt to accept him as a great religious figure in the history of Israel even though they cannot accept him as the Messiah. Further, despite Buber's rejection of Pauline theology and its later development in Christendom, he believed that Jews and Christians should strive to find common ground between their traditions:

> It behooves both you [Christians] and us [Jews] to hold inviolably fast to our own true faith, that is to our own deepest relationship to truth. It behooves both of us to show a religious respect for the true faith of others. This is not what is called 'tolerance'; our task is not to tolerate each other's waywardness but to acknowledge the real relationship in which both stand to the truth. Whenever we both, Christian and Jew, care more for God himself than for our images of God, we are united in the feeling that our Father's house is differently constructed than our human models take it to be.
>
> (Buber, 1948, 40)

Here Buber urged that the adherents of both traditions continue along their separate paths, recognizing the ultimate mystery of faith; yet simultaneously he hoped to evoke a more sympathetic response from the Jewish community to the Christian faith. After twenty centuries of hostility between Christians and Jews, he was convinced that new opportunities existed for positive Jewish–Christian encounter and dialogue.

JACOB KLAUSNER

As Professor at the Hebrew University in Jerusalem, Jacob Klausner explored various aspects of Jewish history, literature and theology as well as Christian origins. In his work, *Jesus of Nazareth*, he attempted to illustrate 'how Judaism differs and remains different for Christianity...every effort has been made to keep it (this work) within the limits of pure scholarship...avoiding those subjective religious and nationalist aims which do not come within the purview of scholarship.' (Klausner, 1964, 10). Yet despite such a commitment to scientific objectivity, Klausner's writings on Jesus and Paul were highly critical of various features of the Christian faith.

The first section of Klausner's study of Jesus and Paul dealt with the history of the period; this was followed by a discussion of sources as well as previous Jewish and Christian scholarly investigations. After this preliminary discussion, Klausner turned to an investigation of the New Testament itself. Regarding John the Baptist, Klausner asserted that the forerunner of Jesus was a Nazarite rather than an Essene. The Essenes might have been a society of Nazarites, but they eliminated all contact with the world, did not welcome disciples, and refrained from any involvement in worldly affairs. Although John the Baptist's life would have mirrored several of these attitudes, his public manner did not conform to the Essene way. Rather John continued a true Jew, imitating the prophets and showing himself akin to them in spirit.

Turning to Jesus, Klausner emphasized that the authors of the Gospels were not interested in history or biography – as a result it is impossible to ascertain a number of features about Jesus' life. Nonetheless, Klausner stressed, it is clear that Jesus was obsessed by the belief that he was the Messiah and his ministry must be viewed from this perspective. The reason Jesus did not announce his messiahship at the beginning was because he did not conform to the traditional image of the Messiah: he was neither a revolutionary, a strict adherent of the Law, nor a kingly figure. Rather he lived as a wandering Galilean teacher, similar to other preachers of the age. Yet unlike these figures in his pronouncements, Jesus emphasized the coming of the messianic age, insisted on the importance of the moral as against the ritual law, utilized parables rather than scriptural exegesis, and performed miracles.

According to Klausner, most of Jesus' disciples were *am ha-aretz* (ignorant members of the community). Because of their lack of knowledge, they were not aware of Jesus' departure from Jewish law and were unable to understand the hostility he aroused among the Pharisees who regarded him as a transgressor. The Sadducees too, Klausner pointed out, were incensed by Jesus' words because of his cleansing of the Temple as well as his reply to them concerning the resurrection of the dead and condemned him. Discussing his trial, Klausner argued that the difference between the court described in the Gospels and the procedure laid down in the Mishnah was due to a difference in the types of court being depicted: the Mishnah portrays a Pharisaic court whereas the Gospels describe a Sadducean court which had ceased to exist by the time the Mishnah was composed. On the basis of this reconstruction, Klausner concluded:

> A few only of the priestly caste had condemned Jesus to death and given him up to Pilate, and only incidentally because of their

annoyance at 'the cleansing of the Temple'...No Jews took any
further part in the actual trial and crucifixion.

(Klausner, 1964, 348)

In his presentation Klausner maintained that Jesus was a typical
Jewish teacher of the first century who fully accepted Jewish Law:
'Jesus was a Jew and a Jew he remained until his last breath. His
one idea was to implant within the nation the idea of the coming of
the Messiah and, by repentance and good works, hasten the end.'
(Klausner, 1964, 368). His ethical pronouncements, Klausner
continued, parallel tannaitic teachings and contain nothing of
originality. Yet Klausner pointed out that Jesus' emphasis on the
moral law was wholly unrealistic – the utopian character of his
preaching is only applicable to the messianic age. Nonetheless,
Klausner admitted that Jesus' message was uplifting for non-Jews:

> For the pagan world, there was a great gain in the belief in the one
> God and in the prophetic ethical teaching which was perpetuated
> in Christianity owing to the teaching of Jesus the Jew.
>
> (Klausner, 1964, 406)

According to Klausner, the strength of Jesus' teaching lay in both
his strength and weaknesses:

> The contradictory traits in his character, its positive and negative
> aspects, his harshness and his gentleness, his clear vision
> combined with his cloudy visionariness – all these united to
> make him a force and an influence, for which history has never
> yet afforded a parallel.
>
> (Klausner, 1964, 411)

Later Jesus' death on the cross added a further dimension to the
meaning of his life and work. Although Jews cannot understand the
religious implications of Jesus' ministry, 'no Jew,' he wrote, 'can
overlook the value of Jesus and his teaching from the point of view
of universal history.' (Klausner, 1964, 413f). In particular, Jesus'
moral code is of paramount importance: 'stripped of its wrappings of
mysticism, the Book of the Ethics of Jesus will be one of the choicest
treasures in the literature of Israel for all time.' (Klausner, 1964, 413f).

Turning to Paul however, Klausner was unable to locate him in
mainstream Judaism. Beginning with a description of the historical

background of the period, Klausner stressed the Hellenistic influence on Paul's thought. In Klausner's view, Paul was not only a mystic and preacher, he was also a clever politician – the early form of Christianity he propounded was nothing more than an adjunct to the religion of the Pharisees and the Essenes. Yet Paul's point of departure consisted in his willingness to adapt his message to a pagan world. Such changes, he argued, could only be done 'by a non-Palestinian Jew, a Hellenistic Jew, who, although he had received some instruction in Palestine, had also imbibed doctrines and learning from the Gentiles...He had to be sufficiently denationalized so as not to care about the damage to the nation caused by the putting aside of the belief in political redemption.' (Klausner, 1964, 300).

As a Hellenistic Jew from Tarsus Paul was able to reinterpret Judaism to fit the needs of the non-Jewish world: Christianity thus became an improved form of Judaism in which gentiles could be included. This Judaism, Klausner maintained, was totally different from the old in its universalistic scope. Paul's spiritualization of Jesus facilitated this transformation – as a result of Paul's encounter with the risen Christ, the crucifixion became the central doctrine in his teaching and Jesus was conceived as sitting on God's right hand. Further, Klausner contended that Jesus never understood the law and found its observances impossibly difficult. Everyone, Paul believed, is a sinner and it was through the atoning death of Jesus that humanity can be saved. All this, Klausner asserted, separated Paul from the faith of his ancestors as did the ethical teaching which sought to replace the moral law which had been abrogated through Jesus' death.

Klausner thus distinguished between Jesus and Paul: Jesus was firmly rooted in the Jewish tradition whereas Paul had deliberately broken away from his ancestral past. Although Jesus had unwittingly altered Judaism, 'the ideological and organic structure of the Christian faith as a religion and as a Church was built by Paul.' (Klausner, 1964, 588). As a Jew, Klausner rejected Paul's reformulation of Judaism. However like other Jewish writers, Klausner perceived that Pauline Christianity has a role to play in the unfolding of God's plan for all people. In Klausner's view, Judaism – rather than Christianity – will become the universal religion; nonetheless, Jewry should acknowledge its debt to Christianity for paving the way for this eventual outcome.

8

Post-Holocaust Jewish Thinkers

The Holocaust has had a profound effect on Jewish attitudes toward Christianity. No longer has it been possible to look forward optimistically to Jewish–Christian encounter as envisioned by previous Jewish thinkers. Nonetheless several writers have continued to explore the relationship between Judaism and Christianity. The German scholar Hans Joachim Schoeps, for example, published a survey of Jewish–Christian dialogue in which he asserted that God has disclosed himself to both communities in different ways – thus it is necessary for Jews and Christians to acknowledge one another's truths. In a different vein the American Jewish theologian Richard Rubenstein reformulated his understanding of God as the result of an encounter with the German Christian pastor Heinrich Grüber, Dean of the Evangelical Church in East and West Berlin. Pondering Grüber's interpretation of the Holocaust, Rubenstein came to the conclusion that he could no longer believe in an interventionist deity. Instead he formulated a mystical theology similar to the systems found in Eastern religions. A very different approach to the Holocaust was undertaken by the American theologian Emil Fackenheim who argued that God had disclosed a new commandment out of the ashes of Auschwitz. According to Fackenheim, both Jews and Christians are now obligated to resist contemporary secularism. As far as Jewry is concerned, Jews are mandated to ensure that Judaism and the Jewish people continue to survive. For two other Jewish theologians – Ignaz Maybaum, and Arthur A. Cohen – Christian motifs and Christian doctrine have provided the basis for their understanding of God's dealings with his chosen people in the Nazi era. In the last few decades then a number of Jewish writers have wrestled with various aspects of Christian teaching in their quest to understand Jewish existence in a post-Holocaust world.

HANS JOACHIM SCHOEPS

In his various writings the German Jewish scholar Hans Joachim Schoeps discussed the thought of Paul, the early development of Christianity, and the history of Jewish–Christian encounter. After the Second World War Schoeps taught at the University of Erlangen; in 1949 a second edition of an earlier work was republished with a new preface in which he reflected on the future of Jewish–Christian encounter after the Holocaust:

> I ask myself today whether the period of religious dialogue may not perhaps be past; whether with these senseless extermina-tions, something quite different has begun. However the case may be, the questions discussed in this book, as well as various essays, was devoted to that theme.
>
> (Schoeps, 1963, xi)

In this book – *Jewish Christian Argument* – Schoeps outlined the history of Jewish–Christian dialogue. Adopting a traditional position, Schoeps asserted that the Hebrew Scriptures is the sole revelation of God to Israel. The *Tanakh*, he asserted, presents God's covenant with his chosen people which 'goes through history ever since that occasion of grace as a covenant community, completely distinct from other nations'. (Schoeps, 1963, 4). Despite this claim, Schoeps acknowledged the Christian conviction that the Church received God's revelation as well – this divine disclosure, he believed, was also valid. Thus, he argued that 'the revelation which has come to each – and come in a different way to each – is truth which comes from God.' (Schoeps, 1963, 8). Both traditions are therefore united in their recognition of the one true God. There is, he stated, only 'one truth, although the modes of participation in the truth differ.' (Schoeps, 1963, 8). According to Schoeps, it is imperative that neither faith should abandon its unique character until the day when all humanity will be united:

> Both are united by one common expectation that the truth, which we do not know, which we can only guess, is yet to come, in that hour when the beginning is swallowed up in the end.
>
> (Schoeps, 1963, 172)

If such progress is to take place, Schoeps argued, it is necessary for both Christians and Jews to acknowledge one another's truths even though the Jewish community will never be able to accept the central tenets of Christian belief. What is possible instead is to discern God's disclosure in the history of Christianity:

> What is basically new – and at the same time also the utmost limit of what is possible – is this: We believe it when they say it. Therein lies the Jewish acknowledgement we have alluded to, namely to grant belief to the Christian witness that God has dealt with the world and a new revelation has taken place outside the covenant with Israel and the revelation to it.
>
> (Schoeps, 1963, 165ff)

Such recognition however does not undermine God's covenant with Israel:

> The recognition of other covenants outside of Israel (the covenant of Christ, and, in principle, that of Mohammed) even fills a gap in Jewish knowledge, since according to Jewish belief, not only Israel, but all mankind belongs to God, and is called on the path to God.
>
> (Schoeps, 1963, 165ff)

In his discussion of Jewish–Christian dialogue, Schoeps was particularly interested in the evolution of early Christianity. In *Theologie und Geschichte des Judenchristentums*, he discussed the relationship between the early Jewish–Christians (Ebionites) and earlier sectarian movements. According to Ebionite theology the Roman victory over the Jewish people in 70 AD was seen as a punishment of the Jewish community for having sanctioned the murder of James, the leader of the Jewish Christian sect, by the Sanhedrin. Further, in Ebionite thought Jesus was understood as the Messiah and a supreme prophet:

> They [Ebionites] associated the teaching of Moses and the teaching of Jesus by means of the idea of primordial religion. Both were sent by God to establish covenants with mankind. Since the two kinds of teaching are identical, God accepts everyone who believes in either of them. Conversion to Jesus,

therefore, is for them precisely the same thing as conversion to God and to the Jewish law.

(Schoeps, 1969, 67)

For the Ebionites, Judaism and Christianity co-exist with parallel covenants. In Ebionite thought Jesus is a purifying prophet, and in his name the Ebionites eliminated the sacrificial cult, the monarchy, female prophecy, false prophesy, the use of anthropomorphisms in Scripture, and reports of unworthy acts by biblical personages. In addition, they added laws and customs, encouraged poverty, established purification through baptism, and prohibited the consumption of meat. Hence the Ebionites stood halfway between Judaism and Christianity, however in time this group was considered heretical by those who shaped the Church.

Schoeps' investigation of the Ebionites was designed to lay the foundation for better Jewish–Christian understanding. Ebionite Christianity, Schoeps argued, could have maintained a link with Judaism if it had become the dominant form of the Christian faith. However because of Paul's influence, this did not occur – instead Pauline Christianity gained ascendancy. As Schoeps explained, Paul believed that all who accepted the resurrected Christ would be spiritually resurrected; as a result, the earthly Jesus receded in importance and was replaced by a heavenly Saviour. Paul's messianic theology, Schoeps continued, provided a combination of prominent Jewish motifs – the suffering Messiah, the dying Messiah, the warrior Messiah, and the spiritual Messiah – with the added dimension of divinity. Yet despite such a reliance on Jewish ideas, such a transformation was utterly unacceptable for most Jews.

Concerning Paul's conception of the sacrificial death of Jesus, Paul again appealed to Jewish motifs. In his writing he utilized the themes of the atoning efficacy of the sufferings of the righteous, the suffering of the Messiah and the sacrifice of Isaac. He 'combined these conceptions with the Messianically understood *Akedath Isaac* (sacrifice of Isaac) in such a way as to transfer the story from Abraham and Isaac to the eternal God Himself and His Incarnate Son, and thus exalted the Messiah beyond all human proportions to the status of real divinity – this is the radically un-Jewish element in the thought of the apostle'. (Schoeps, 1961, 158). Since such a conception was a radical departure from Jewish theology, it was vigorously opposed by both Jews as well as the early Jewish Christians.

Turning to Paul's view of the Law, Schoeps noted that other Jewish messianic groups similarly expected the Jewish legal system to be abolished after the coming of the Messiah. Yet Paul's understanding of the Law was not acceptable to mainstream Judaism: 'The Pauline inference that the law, which could not prevent universal sinfulness, and on the basis of which no man could be justified by his works, is a law unto death, is one which no Jew could draw.' (Schoeps, 1961, 175). Paul's most serious departure from Jewish teaching was his contention that the Law was intended to increase sinfulness – such a conception was equally unacceptable to Jewry:

> Every child of the Jews, whether the Diaspora or the Judaism of Palestine is in question, knows that the law had no other purpose than that of being given by God in order to be kept and not transgressed, in order to increase resistance to sin and not augment sin.
>
> (Schoeps, 1961, 194f)

In his writings then Schoeps sought to illustrate the common ground between Judaism and early Christianity. His exploration of Ebionite theology was an attempt to pave the way for a more sympathetic Jewish understanding of the origins of the Christian faith. In Schoeps' view, it was the influence of Pauline thought which led to the breach between these two faiths. What is currently required is for Jews to recapture the original message of the Church – in this way Jews and Christians can be reconciled in a post-Holocaust world. Thus presupposing a form of Jewish Inclusivism, Schoeps argued that although Judaism is the fullest disclosure of divine revelation, God also made himself manifest to the Christian community in a parallel covenant.

RICHARD RUBENSTEIN

The Holocaust had a profound impact on subsequent Jewish–Christian dialogue. No longer has it been possible to look forward optimistically to positive Jewish–Christian encounter – instead the death camps have cast a shadow over all efforts to achieve understanding between Christians and Jews. In the early 1960s however the American Jewish theologian Richard Rubenstein attempted to engage in Jewish–Christian dialogue on German soil. In *After Auschwitz* Rubenstein explained that his perception of the Holocaust was deeply influenced by an encounter with a distinguished German pastor, Heinrich Grüber, Dean of the Evangelical Church in East and West Berlin.

In August 1961 Rubenstein had scheduled a research trip to West Germany. On 13 August the wall between East and West Berlin was erected which caused an international crisis. Rubenstein decided to postpone his visit until 15 August; when he arrived in Bonn, he was invited by the Press and Information Office of the Federal Republic to fly to Berlin. When he arrived he attended a mass rally addressed by the mayor of Berlin, Willy Brandt, and visited East Berlin. In this atmosphere Rubenstein interviewed Dean Grüber at his home in the West Berlin suburb of Dahlem.

During the Second World War Grüber helped baptize Jews and opposed the anti-Semitic programme of the Nazis. As a result, he was incarcerated in Sachsenhausen concentration camp. In 1961 he was the only German to testify at the trial of Adolf Eichmann. In his conversation with Rubenstein, the Dean affirmed that God was active in history and was responsible for the Holocaust. Quoting Psalm 44:22 'For thy sake are we slaughtered every day.' Grüber explained that for some reason, it was part of God's plan that the Jews died. Comparing the terrible events of the Nazi regime with contemporary circumstances, he declared:

> At different times, God uses different peoples as his whip against his own people, the Jews, but those whom he uses will be punished far worse than the people of the Lord...I know that God is punishing us because we have been the whip against Israel. In 1938 we smashed the synagogues; in 1945 our churches were smashed by the bombs. In 1938 we sent the Jews out to be homeless; since 1945 fifteen million Germans have experienced homelessness.
>
> (Rubinstein, 1992, 10)

Grüber believed that Hitler's actions were immoral and that he would be punished. Though he did not explain why God punished the Jews, Rubenstein concluded that for Grüber it was because of their unwillingness to recognize Jesus as their Saviour. This was certainly the view of the German Ecumenical Church three years after the war – in 1948 at a meeting in Darmstadt the Church asserted that the Holocaust was a divine punishment visited upon the Jews, and they called upon the Jewish community to cease their rejection of Jesus Christ.

Though Rubenstein was shocked by Grüber's words, he recognized that there was nothing new in this attempt to understand history as the unfolding of God's plan. A parallel interpretation of Jewish history was held by the biblical prophets, the rabbis, and the Church Fathers. Nevertheless, Rubenstein had never before heard the argument applied to the events of the modern world. Yet as he explained in *After Auschwitz*, there was no reason to reject its logic:

> Given the Judeo-Christian conception so strong in Scripture, that God is the ultimate actor in the historical drama, no other theological interpretation of the death of six million Jews is tenable...If one views all time and history through the perspective of the Christ, one would ultimately have to assert that God caused the Jews to be exterminated by the Nazis because of their continuing failure to confess and acknowledge the Christ. If one shared Rabban Johanan ben Zakkai's view, one would be drawn to assert that the Jewish people had been exterminated because of their failure to comply with the Lord's commandments as these had been enjoined in the Torah.
>
> (Rubinstein, 1992, 17)

When Rubenstein left Grüber's house, he was convinced that he could not avoid the issue of God's relation to the Holocaust. Though Grüber's view of God as involved in human history was in harmony with Scripture, Rubenstein could not believe in such a divine being. It seemed amazing to him that Jewish theologians still subscribed to the belief in an omnipotent, beneficent God after the death camps. Traditional Jewish theology maintains that God is the ultimate actor in history – it interprets every tragedy as God's punishment for Israel's sinfulness. But Rubenstein was unable to see how this position could be maintained without viewing Hitler as an instrument of His will:

> The agony of European Jewry cannot be likened to the testing of Job. To see any purpose in the death camps, the traditional believer is forced to regard the most demonic, anti-human

explosion in all history as a meaningful expression of God's purposes. The idea is simply too obscene for me to accept.

(Rubinstein, 1966, 153)

According to Rubenstein, a void now exists where once the Jewish people experienced God's presence. This demythologizing of the Jewish tradition is, he argued, acknowledged in contemporary Jewish life even if it is not made explicit in Jewish theology. In the diaspora and in Israel the myth of an omnipotent God of history is effectively repudiated in the lives of most Jewish people. After the Nazi period, life is lived and enjoyed on its own terms without any superordinate values or special theological relationship.

Though Rubenstein rejected the image of God in the Hebrew Scriptures, he insisted that it would be a mistake to construe his position as atheism – what he wished to illustrate is that we live in the time of the death of God. He is compelled to use terminology because it conveys the contemporary Jewish experience of God's absence:

When I say we live in the time of the death of God, I mean that the thread uniting God and man, Heaven and earth has been broken. We stand in a cold, silent, unfeeling cosmos, unaided by any powerful power beyond our own resources. After Auschwitz, what else can a Jew say about God?

(Rubinstein, 1966, 151–2)

In *Approaches to Auschwitz*, his most recent study of the Holocaust written with the Christian theologian John Roth, Rubenstein explained that his theological view today is akin to mystical religion – he no longer regards the universe as cold and unfeeling. His earlier views in *After Auschwitz* should be seen as the response of an assimilated Jew to the Jewish tradition after the extermination of millions of Jews. His position then was understandably bleak; yet today he would balance the elements of creativeness and love in the cosmos more evenly with those of destruction and hate than he was prepared to do in 1966. As Rubenstein came into contact with the civilizations and religions of Asia since the publication of After Auschwitz, he began to formulate a mystical theology similar to the mysticism found in Buddhism and Hegelian thought. In mysticism Rubenstein found a God whom he could affirm after the Holocaust – this view has replaced his earlier emphasis on the coldness and silence of the cosmos. This notion of God, he insisted, is meaningful after the death of the God-who-acts-in-history. It is an ancient conception with deep roots in Western and Oriental mysticism. According to this view, God is the Holy Nothingness. As such he is the ground and source of everything. He is not a void; rather such a God is an individual plenum, so rich that all existence is derived from his very essence. He is superfluity of being rather than absence of being.

Rubenstein's use of the term 'Nothingness' rests in part upon the ancient observation that all definitions of finite entities involve negation. The infinite God cannot be defined – he is in no sense a thing bearing any resemblance to finite beings. Mystics have also spoken of God as the primary ground, the dark unnameable abyss out of which the empirical world emerged. In all the major world religions, sages have attempted to communicate the divine mystery by the use of similar images. 'Perhaps the best available metaphor for the concept of God as the Holy Nothingness,' Rubenstein wrote, 'is that God is the ocean and we are the waves. In some sense each wave has its moment in which it is distinguishable, as a somewhat separate entity. Nevertheless, no wave is entirely distinct from the ocean which is the substantial ground.' (Rubinstein, 1987, 316). In mysticism then Rubenstein has found the God whom he can affirm after Auschwitz, even though such a conception is far removed from the biblical and rabbinic view of a transcendental God who created and sustains the universe and providentially watches over his chosen people.

EMIL FACKENHEIM

Born in Germany in 1915, the Jewish theologian Emil Fackenheim emigrated to Canada in 1940 and subsequently taught at the University of Toronto. Prior to the Six Day War, Fackenheim expressed concern about the possibilities of Jewish–Christian dialogue. According to Fackenheim, the Christian has been unwilling to understand Jewish existence – instead of seeing a living religion, he envisions Judaism as a fossil. In addition, many Christians have been unable to accept Israel as a modern state. These factors, as well as the Christian unwillingness to accept responsibility for the Holocaust, are major obstacles to positive Jewish–Christian encounter.

Despite these difficulties, Fackenheim stressed that it is vital for Jews and Christians to unite in facing the challenge of modern secular society. In formulating this common policy, Fackenheim reflected on the theological implications of the Holocaust. In a wide range of writings, Fackenheim has sought to provide an authentic response to the horrors of the Nazi period. According to Fackenheim, the Holocaust was a unique event. Even the term 'genocide' does not capture the most important aspects of this calamity. There are two central factors, he argued, which distinguish this event from other occurrences. First, six million Jews were murdered not because of their religious beliefs, but because their grandparents continued to see themselves within the Jewish covenant. And second, the process of killing was seen as an end in itself; unlike previous massacres, Jews did not face death in order to bear witness to their faith. The uniqueness of the Holocaust is thus of central importance to Fackenheim because of the way in which the Nazis defined Jewishness in order to rid Europe of Jewry. Killing Jews became a goal in itself, and such an intention is an example of what Fackenheim calls 'radical evil'. This is what differentiates the Holocaust from all other acts of genocide in which there was a rational goal. Even though modern Jews might wish to divorce the Holocaust from previous Jewish history, this is impossible – it serves as a terrifying reminder that the Jew cannot escape his own tragedy.

In Fackenheim's view God's presence was manifest in the death camps just as he revealed himself in ancient times. Just as the root experience of God's presence at Mount Sinai resulted in a series of divine commands, so in the death camps God revealed a further commandment to his chosen people. This 614th commandment – added to the 613 commandments contained in the Torah – is directed to the post Holocaust Jewish community. In *God's Presence in History: Jewish Affirmations and Philosophical Reflections*, he gave a full explanation of this decree:

Jews are forbidden to hand Hitler posthumous victories. They are commanded to survive as Jews, lest the Jewish people perish. They are commanded to remember the victims of Auschwitz lest their memory perish. They are forbidden to despair of man and his world, and to escape into either cynicism or other-worldliness, lest they co-operate in delivering the world over to the forces of Auschwitz. Finally, they are forbidden to despair of the God of Israel, lest Judaism perish...A Jew may not respond to Hitler's attempt to destroy Judaism by himself co-operating in its destruction. In ancient times, the unthinkable Jewish sin was idolatry. Today, it is to respond to Hitler by doing his work.

(Cohn-Sherbok, 1989, 46)

According to Fackenheim, it is a sacred duty to remember the Holocaust. The intention of the Nazis to eliminate all Jews – no survivor was to be left to tell the story of the horrors that took place. They were making as sure as possible that every trace of memory would be wiped out. Millions would be as though they had never been. The Commanding Voice of Auschwitz demands that those who perished must never be forgotten. It is a holy duty to remember and tell the tale – such an obligation is not negotiable. Fackenheim further insisted that the Commanding Voice of Auschwitz also bids Jews not to abandon the world to the forces of darkness. Instead they must continue to work for a more humane society. They must not despair of the world because of the events of the Nazi period; nor should they abandon the age-old identification with the poor and the persecuted. It is because of the uniqueness of Auschwitz and their role as Jews that they must identify with all humanity.

In a later work, *To Mend the World: Foundations of Future Jewish Thought*, Fackenheim argued that the Nazi regime was intent on making individuals *Muselmanner* (people who are dead while alive). Yet despite this plan, some inmates did resist. For Fackenheim such acts of resistance constitute the religious response to Auschwitz and the beginning of *tikkun* (cosmic repair). Fackenheim pointed out that rebellion in the camps took many forms: some victims consciously prevented themselves from becoming *Muselmanner*; pregnant women refused to abort their pregnancies so that their children could survive; Jewish partisans took to the woods to fight the Nazis; Hasidic Jews prayed when forbidden to do so. Although such gestures were infrequent, they demonstrate that there were some prisoners who resisted against hopeless odds – their heroism shows that the logic of destruction can be thwarted.

Fackenheim maintained that the Holocaust must continue to be resisted in contemporary society. Civilization now includes death camps and *Muselmanner*; those who understand what took place in the Holocaust cannot overlook the rationally organized, systematic, excremental assault on the Jewish people. As a consequence, resistance to the Holocaust and the quest for *tikkun* have become never-ending imperatives. Further, Fackenheim contended that only as a result of the deed of resistance can resisting thought be effective. In the case of those inmates who had the courage to act, thought and action were united. Just as the Holocaust was a *novum* in history, so too this resistance was a *novum* – it was a way of being and a way of thought. Here Fackenheim cited the example of Pelagia Lewinska, a Polish Catholic, who illuminatingly represents such a combination of thought and deed:

> At the outset the living places, the ditches, the mud, the piles of excrement behind the blocks, had appalled me with their horrific filth...and then I saw the light! I saw that it was not a question of disorder or lack of organization but that, on the contrary, a very thoroughly considered conscious idea was in the back of the camp's existence. They had condemned us to die in our own filth, to drown in mud, in our own excrement. They wished to abase us, to destroy our human dignity, to efface every vestige of humanity...to fill us with horror and contempt towards ourselves and our fellows...From the instant when I grasped the motivating principle...it was as if I had been awakened from a dream...I felt under order to live...And if I did die in Auschwitz, it would be as a human being, I would hold on to my dignity. I was not going to become the contemptible, disgusting brute my enemy wished me to be...And a terrible struggle began which went on day and night.
>
> (Fackenheim, 1982, 250)

For Fackenheim such commitment is of central importance. Lewinska – as a Catholic – felt obliged to resist and endure – her experience is evidence of God's commanding voice. Fackenheim believed that the rupture caused by the Holocaust must be mended by similar acts of *tikkun*. Previously Jewish mysticism described the disasters that afflicted Jewry as catastrophes within the Godhead; such rupture separated God from himself. According to the mystics, reconciliation in the heavenly and earthly spheres can only be attained through prayer and ritual observance. In the modern world, however, acts of resistance must take the place of this religious activity. For Fackenheim the most profound reaction to the Holocaust is the establishment of a Jewish homeland for the survivors of the camps. In a Jewish state Jews are able to find a refuge and ensure that such catastrophes are never repeated. Fackenheim argued that post-Holocaust *tikkun* can most significantly take place in Israel since there Jews are able to defend themselves without depending on others. Such *tikkun* involves religious as well as secular Jews who share a common inheritance – together they can ensure Jewish survival in a world torn by the events of the Nazi period.

IGNAZ MAYBAUM

In formulating a response to the Holocaust, the British Reform theologian Ignaz Maybaum utilized biblical as well as Christian imagery in his explanation of divine providence. According to Maybaum, the Holocaust was the result of God's will. In the case of the exodus from Egypt, God acted with trials, signs, wonders, war, a mighty hand, an outstretched arm, and great terrors (Deuteronomy 4:32). For Maybaum, the third *churban* (event of utter destructiveness) – the Holocaust – was full of terror. In this tragedy the servant-of-God passages in the Book of Isaiah provide the framework for comprehending God's plan for humanity. In Auschwitz, Maybaum maintained, Jews suffered vicarious death for the sins of all people. Of the martyr-servant it is written: 'Behold, my servant shall succeed, he shall be exalted and lifted up, and shall be very high' (Isaiah 52:13). Those who died in the gas chambers are similarly exalted. Leo Baeck, the distinguished Reform rabbi and leader of German Jewry, for example, came out from Thereseinstadt and brought with him a message in which he interpreted the Book of Daniel. Here the author who lived at the time of religious persecution asked: what happens to those who died and will not see the liberation, soon and surely to come? The answer was that they do not die into the grave, they die into the eternity of God.

In his discussion of the role of the Jewish people in God's plan for humanity, Maybaum contended that Auschwitz is the twentieth century Calvary of the Jewish people. The Golgotha of modern mankind is Auschwitz – the Cross has been replaced by the gas chamber. According to Maybaum, the Golgotha of Auschwitz was nothing other than a place of slaughter where pagans discarded their Christian teachings: 'Golgotha with Christianity absenting itself became a place of skulls. Auschwitz is the pagan Golgotha of our time.' (Maybaum, 1965, 80). Again he wrote: 'A Christianity

withdrawn from the responsibility of history shares the responsibility for the twentieth-century Golgotha of six million Jews.'
(Maybaum, 1965, 80). Thus despite the sincere fellowship expressed
by many Christians towards Jews today, it must not be forgotten
that the Church was largely a silent bystander as millions of Jews
were murdered in the death camps.

Maybaum was also anxious to connect the martyrdom of the
victims of Nazi persecution with the sacrificial system of ancient
Israel. The ceremony of atonement, he pointed out, was a central
part of the Temple cult. In Scripture we read about the High Priest,
animal sacrifice, and the blood of the offering which was sprinkled
on the altar. After this ceremony the High Priest, his family and all
the people praised the Lord and then prayed, 'Blessed be the name
of the glory of his Kingdom for ever.' In Auschwitz the Jewish
people were both the High Priest and the sacrificial lamb. The
victims died because of the sins of others. As a result, the world is
cleaner because the passion of savagery was spent and because
modern views of technical progress have revealed their nihilism
leading to destruction. The work of atonement had been fulfilled. In
the tragedy of Auschwitz the Jewish people were victimized and
through this vicarious suffering atonement has been granted to
future generations.

In formulating this conception of sacrificial atonement Maybaum
pointed out that the modern age is a time of martyrdom. Once the
death of those who were murdered by the Nazis is understood as
holy martyrdom, it is possible to return to God. The result of those
murders was to bring God back to the world which had forsaken
him. In the Hebrew Bible, the servant is the witness who makes the
martyrdom visible. The martyrdom of six million Jews is therefore
not simply a national catastrophe – it is an assault against humanity.
The Jew represents humankind – in the words of the medieval
philosopher Judah Halevi the Jew without mankind is like the heart
in the body. If the heart is sick, the limbs become weak and decay.
The pogrom of Kristallnacht was the prelude to this calamity, and
disaster followed which devastated the whole world. Eastern
Europe and parts of Russia were decimated; German cities were in
ruins; Great Britain was bombed as was Pearl Harbor; the atomic
bomb was dropped on Hiroshima. This apocalyptic Holocaust
began with the Nazis' programme of anti-Semitism.

Yet those who died were only one-third of the Jewish nation. The
surviving two-thirds constitute the 'Remnant'. For Maybaum the

churban brought about progress through sacrifice. But what kind of development took place? Maybaum insisted that this catastrophe brought about an end to the medieval period. The structure of medieval society which survived for centuries in Eastern Europe was eliminated. Hitler – as an instrument of God's will – did what should have been done by others. The old order of Eastern European Jewry was exterminated in the gas chambers; after Auschwitz this large segment of the Jewish people who lived an essentially medieval lifestyle came to an end.

In the Middle Ages lord and vassal were bound together by an authoritarian hierarchy. This system of social differentiation created a pyramid in which inequality became the primary social binding force. The Caesar as pope or emperor made the Middle Ages the heir of Roman imperialism. In this environment there was simply no place for Jewry. Jews were the killers of Christ, and thus providentially destined to be punished for their sin. Hitler was viewed by many as a crusader – Auschwitz was the place where the directors of the Inquisition did their work in the midst of the twentieth century. Yet Hitler accomplished what the progressives should have done – he destroyed the old Europe.

The end of the Middle Ages means the passing of Jewish submission. It is not merely small isolated groups of the Jewish nation who have been freed, but the whole of the Jewish community is now Westernized. Jewry can emancipate itself from the enforced compliance of Jewish religious life and dismiss the medieval mentality which separated one community from another, making Zionism necessary. While remaining loyal to the citizens of Israel, diaspora Jewry can realize that the Holy Land is not a country on the shores of the Mediterranean; it is rather humanity's future. The exodus from the Middle Ages is thus assured. In Western democracies Jew and Christian meet as equals; they are to be treated in the same fashion before the law. Such equality breaks down the barriers between Jew and non-Jew and offers to them both an opportunity to enrich the world in different ways. The Jewish people has forged its spears into ploughshares and now sees the betterment of humanity as its goal.

In replacing the medieval with the modern approach, contemporary Jewish historiography put an end to the concept of history as a long-drawn-out story of miracles and a continuous chain of legends about saintly individuals. Historical reality became the place where God encountered human beings. The medieval dream has thus ended. Western men and women now take history seriously. In this regard they have moved closer to the Hebrew Bible than was possible in a medieval atmosphere. Westernized individuals have a dominant place on the stage of history. The remnant of the Jewish nation – the survivors of the third *churban* – have become increasingly Westernized, and with the rise of Western civilization the Jew will arise too. Out of the depths into which the catastrophe of our time plunged the Jewish people, there is hope for the future.

It is the prophetic task of the Jewish nation to interpret Auschwitz as an awful portent in the exodus from the past into the future. In the post-*churban* era, Western civilization can be the mediating agent which brings to humanity what God has planned: justice, kindness and peace. Through the Jewish enlightenment movement, Zionism and socialism, Jews previously attempted to bring Western ideas and the blessings of a Western way of life to East European Jewry. This task failed – yet the terrible efficiency of Auschwitz achieved this goal. As Jews say farewell to the long tradition of the Jewish people in the Middle Ages, they must be sustained by prophetic faith. Archaic traditions cannot serve them on their journey into the future. Only listening to God can help them after the breakdown of their faithfully preserved heritage. In the hour of the *churban*, the great and awful destruction of the medieval world, God calls the Jewish people as he did in ancient times: 'Prepare to meet thy God, O Israel.' (Amos 4:12).

ARTHUR A. COHEN

Another post-Holocaust Jewish thinker who was influenced by Christian theology was the Conservative rabbi and theologian Arthur A. Cohen. To differentiate the Holocaust from other events, Cohen referred to the mass murder of European Jewry as the *Tremendum*. The use of this term is based on the German Protestant theologian Rudolf Otto's *The Idea of the Holy* in which the Holy is viewed as the dimension of God's presence. For Otto, God is near and present, but no less terrifying and unfathomable. He is thus described as the *Mysterium Tremendum* – the utter mystery. The phenomenology of the Holy begins with the recognition of the terror-mystery of God which is modified by the traditional modes of mercy, love and justice until the shattering presence becomes the still, small voice. According to Cohen, the counter to the *Mysterium Tremendum* is the human *Tremendum*:

> The enormity of an infinitized man, who no longer seems to fear death or, perhaps more to the point, fears it so completely, denies death so mightily, that the only patent of his refutation and denial is to build a mountain of corpses to the divinity of the dead, to placate death by the magic of endless murder.
>
> (Cohen, 1981, 18–19)

The death camps are the *Tremendum* – they are the monument of the orgastic celebration of death. Arguably the Jew is the ideal victim because his survival is a celebration of the tenacity of life. Jewish converts who adopted other faiths have maintained that Judaism has lost its vitality. The Jew is conceived as dead. Thus the living Jew must die so that the non-Jew can be saved. In this regard Cohen referred to Martin Buber's view that there is no caesura in the history of the Jewish people. According to Buber, there is no gap to be filled by the Holy Spirit. Cohen agreed with this interpretation of Jewish experience, yet he argued it fails to take account of the underside of history – the corrupting caesura. 'For the Holy,' he wrote, 'there may be no caesura, but the unholy its name is caesura.' (Cohen, 1981, 20). In the time of the human *Tremendum*, time and causality are interrupted. At that moment the demonic tears the skein of events apart – then human beings are forced to look into the abyss.

For the Jewish community this is not a new experience. The destruction of the Temple and the obliteration of the nation was an abyss. There was a caesura: 'The abyss opened and the Jews crossed the abyss by affirming their guilt, denying the abyss, and taking upon themselves responsibility for the demonic.' (Cohen, 1981, 21). The expulsion of the Jews from Spain was another caesura – again the abyss opened and the Jews reaffirmed their guilt. They transformed the event into an end-time of history and the beginning of an unseen mystical order. The third caesura of the demonic is the Holocaust. However, it is no longer possible to respond as did survivors of the first caesura. Jews were not responsible for the devastation that befell them during the Nazi era. Nor should modern Jews respond as did the survivors of the second abyss. The kabbalistic interpretation of Spanish exile and the destruction of Sephardic Jewry is not a viable approach for contemporary Judaism. The third abyss should be confronted neither with guilt nor hope.

The abyss of the death camps cannot be transcended; it must be inspected fully. A descent deep into its midst must be attempted. For the Jew the death camps are historically real. Jews are obliged to hear the witness as though they were themselves witness. They must experience the *Tremendum* just as in every generation the Jewish community is obligated at Passover to consider that they themselves were redeemed from Egypt. It is not enough to make liturgy and midrash out of the Holocaust – Jews must create a new language in which to speak of this break in history. By separating the *Tremendum* from all things and descending into the abyss, it should be possible to rejoin it to the whole experience of mankind.

According to Cohen, the *Tremendum* casts doubt on traditional Jewish theism – it requires a response that takes account of the horrors of the death camps. Before the Holocaust the suppositions of traditional Judaism had already been under attack. Only by appealing to mystery could Jewish thinkers reconcile the doctrine of a transcendental God with the scriptural presentation of a loving, merciful and just redeemer. The *Tremendum* exacerbates this theological perplexity: it is necessary today to account for the murder of six million Jews. In confronting this issue Cohen redefined the reality of God and his relation to the world.

Cohen pointed out that the neo-Orthodox theologians of earlier decades appealed to the concept of paradox to account for God's ways. Yet these formulations were restricted by defining God as the pre-eminent object of wonder, and the existential situation of the believer as one who faithfully eschewed philosophical questioning. Such neo-Orthodoxy, however, is unsatisfactory since it situates the *Tremendum* as the counter of an absent or hidden God. It enables 'the immensity of the one to pass the mystery of the other in the dark night of this century without compelling them to their dreadful confrontation'. (Cohn-Sherbok, 1989, 75). For Cohen what is needed instead is a constructive theology which has several characteristics. First, the God who is affirmed must abide in a universe where history is scarred by genuine evil. Second, the relation of God and creation must include demonic structures – unredeemable events must be seen as meaningful and valuable. Finally, the reality of God cannot be isolated from God's involvement in history.

The *Tremendum* obliges Jews to accept the kabbalistic belief that God was enlivened by the spark of non-being. The cosmogony of the kabbalah asserts that there are scaled emissions of being which derive their nature and vitality from God; they emerge from the lowest to highest, linked by the complexity of their own structure to the divine structure. They are imperfect according to their adhesion to the divine image. It is only through such kabbalistic notions, Cohen insisted, that it is possible to make sense of the events of the Nazi era. The divine word is the origin of the creation of the void. As the whole of the divine nature is enlarged by the presence of non-being, so creation is a necessity within God as is freedom of the will in man. The divine overflows. What is absolute in God is seen by us under the aspect of his plentitude. New forms, new beginnings, new creations are already within God in the eternal Now. Their creative process is complemented by human beings whose essential character is freedom. God engenders possibility, but humans are free to act.

In the past Jews believed that God acts in history. Thus they proclaim that he redeemed them from Egyptian bondage. For Cohen, however, 'God is not the strategist of our particularities or of our historical condition but rather the mystery of our futurity, always our *posse*, never our acts.' (Cohen, 1981, 97). God, he contended, must not be seen as an interferer, but as the hope of our futurity. He is not the cause of historical events, nor indifferent to history. Rather the divine life is a filament within the historical. Yet historical occurrences are the domain of human freedom. The *Tremendum* therefore means that human beings, not God, render the filament incandescent or burns it out:

Man can obscure, eclipse, burn out the divine filament...it is this which is meant by the abyss of the historical, the demonic, the *Tremendum*.

(Cohen, 1981, 98)

Previously Jews conceived of history as the arena for God's action. Events were viewed as means towards the fulfilment of God's eternal providential plan. History was thus the manifestation of God's will in which there would be the unfolding of the *eschaton*. The historical is in this view the scene for the manifestation of God's kingdom in which the Jewish people play a central role. But the Jew today is not the same as the Jew of yesterday or the Jew at Sinai. The belief that God is the sole agency in the universe – its king, ruler and authority – is no longer feasible. It is a mistake to think that the only agent is the divine expansion.

According to Cohen, the traditional conception of God's relation to the world must be transcended. Historical events should be seen as the result of human freedom rather than the effect of divine causality. In this light the *Tremendum* is a human volcano which has scorched the entire earth. It is like a 'dead' volcano, terrifying in its aspect but silent, monstrous in its gaping, raw in the entrails, a visible reminder of fire and magma, but now a quiet, immovable presence, yawning over the lives of man.' (Cohen, 1981, 108–9). This destruction was a caesura in the life of the nation and as such calls for a reassessment of the classical notion of an interruptive God who guides the course of events. For Cohen the Holocaust was a human creation rather than part of God's providential plan. Thus it is ultimately human beings – not God – who should be held responsible for the tragedy that befell European Jewry.

9
Jewish Religious Pluralism

Throughout history Judaism has adopted a largely tolerant attitude toward other faiths. In biblical times the religion of Israel was Exclusivist in orientation; nonetheless pagan people were not condemned for their beliefs and practices. Further, the prophets believed that in the final days all the nations of the world would recognise that the God of Israel is the Lord of creation. During the rabbinic period all attitudes of tolerance continued to animate Jewish life; according to the rabbis all non-Jews who follow the Noahide laws are acceptable to God. A number of medievalists continued this tradition, and in the modern period there has been an increasing acknowledgement of the integrity of other faiths, particularly Christianity. In nearly all cases Jewish thinkers have espoused various forms of Inclusivism. However, in the modern world Jewry needs to adopt an even more open stance toward the world's religions – what is required today is a Copernican shift from Inclusivism to Pluralism in which God, rather than Judaism, is at the centre of the universe of faiths. Such a Pluralist position would enable Jews to affirm the uniqueness of their faith while urging them to recognize the integrity of other traditions. The theology lying behind this shift from Inclusivism to Pluralism is based on the distinction between Reality as it is in itself and the Real as perceived. From a Pluralist perspective, the truth claims of Judaism – as well as the truth claims of other religions – should be regarded as human constructions rather than universal absolutes embodying divine truth. Within such a Pluralistic framework it is impossible to assert that Judaism is the superior religion; rather it must be seen simply as one among many religious systems of conceptualization. The theological implications of such a reorientation are very great: from a Pluralistic standpoint the traditional doctrines of the Jewish faith should be viewed as religious hypothesis rather than certain knowledge.

JUDAISM AND OTHER RELIGIONS

From this survey of past attitudes toward other religions, it is evident that Judaism has adopted a relatively tolerant attitude through the ages. In the biblical period ancient Israelites were encouraged to view the gods of other peoples as non-entities. In this respect ancient Israelite faith was Exclusivist in orientation. Yet foreign peoples were not condemned for their pagan practices. Although the religion of the Jewish people was perceived as the one true faith, there was no harsh condemnation of idolatry. Furthermore, it was the conviction of the prophets that in the end of days all nations would recognize that the God of the Israelites was the Lord of the universe. Thus, there was no compulsion to missionise among non-believers. There was hope even for pagan peoples in the unfolding of God's plan of salvation.

In the rabbinic period this tradition of tolerance continued to animate Jewish life. According to the rabbis, all non-Jews who follow the Noahide Laws are viewed as acceptable to God. In this context even those who engage in polytheistic practices are admissible as long as the gods they worship are conceived as symbolically pointing to the one God. Here in these rabbinic sources is the beginning of a form of Inclusivism in which foreign peoples – despite their seeming polytheism – were seen as 'anonymous monotheists'. In the medieval period such writers as Rabbenu Tam applied this rabbinic conception of symbolic intermediacy to Christian believers. In his opinion Christianity is not idolatry since Christians are monotheists despite their belief in the Trinity. Other writers such as Judah Halevi formulated an even more tolerant form of Jewish Inclusivism: for these thinkers Christians as well as Muslims play an important role in God's plan for humanity by spreading the message of monotheism.

Such a positive stance toward other faiths continued into the early modern period due to the impact of the Enlightenment. In the eighteenth century the Jewish philosopher Moses Mendelssohn argued that the Jewish people were the recipients of a divine revelation consisting of ritual and moral law. Nevertheless Mendelssohn was convinced that God's reality can be discerned through human reason. Thus all human beings – regardless of their religious persuasion – are capable of discerning God's nature and activity. During this period other thinkers offered a sympathetic appreciation of Christianity while at the same time adhering to the belief that

Judaism is the superior religion. The French scholar Joseph Salvador for example, believed that in the future Christians would help to bring about a new philosophical religion resembling Judaism; in this respect his positive evaluation of Christianity provided a form of Jewish Inclusivism tempered by the scientific spirit of the age. Similarly the German reform rabbi Abraham Geiger argued that Christianity embraces God's revelation to his chosen people, yet Judaism constitutes the ideal faith for the modern age.

During the age of Emancipation Jewish thinkers grappled with the currents of Western philosophical thought and in their different ways offered a positive evaluation of both Christianity and Islam. Pre-eminent among nineteenth-century Jewish writers the German theologian Samuel Hirsch maintained that throughout history Judaism struggled to overcome the threat of paganism. According to Hirsch, in this quest Christianity has an important role; however the Jewish faith as the purest form of monotheism is humanity's ultimate hope for the future. A similar form of Jewish Inclusivism was espoused by the German reform rabbi Solomon Formstecher who argued that even though Judaism is the ultimate form of the religious life, Christianity and Islam play an important part in the unfolding of God's plan. Such a view was also advanced by another German thinker of this age, Solomon Ludwig Steinheim, who viewed Christianity as furthering God's eschatological scheme. An even more positive assessment of Christianity was fostered by the British Jewish writer Claude Montefiore who stressed that God reveals himself in different ways throughout history. For Montefiore the Christian faith is one such disclosure, and Jews can be enlightened by a knowledge of the New Testament. In Montefiore's work there is thus a full endorsement of Judaism with tentative steps toward the formulation of a Pluralist stance.

The quest to explore the origins of Christianity, its subsequent development, and the relationship between the Jewish and Christian faith was a major concern of a number of modern Jewish thinkers. The Czech writer Max Brod for example admired Jesus as a Jewish preacher, yet he was critical of Paul's transformation of the Christian faith. According to Brod, Christianity was corrupted through the centuries by the infusion of pagan elements. In his opinion, Judaism is the only hope for the future. Such an Inclusivist stance was further elaborated by the German Jewish theologian Franz Rosenzweig who regarded Christianity as fulfilling a crucial role in spreading the message of monotheism to all peoples. A similar endorsement of the Christian faith was affirmed by the German Jewish leader Leo Baeck who, like other Jewish writers before him, attempted to reclaim Jesus as an authentic Jewish figure despite his criticism of Pauline Christianity and its negative impact on the growth of Christian theology. Likewise the German Jewish theologian Martin Buber admired Jesus as a great religious teacher. In the same fashion the biblical scholar Jacob Klausner regarded Jesus as a typical Jewish figure of the 1st century who should evoke esteem from the Jewish community. In Klausner's opinion, Judaism will eventually become the religion for all people; nevertheless Jews should acknowledge their debt to Christianity for paving the way for this outcome.

Such reflections about the relationship between Judaism and Christianity were eclipsed by the Holocaust. With rare exceptions – such as the writings of Hans Joachim Schoeps – it was no longer possible for Jews to foster such a positive assessment of Christian origins and the role of Christianity in the unfolding of God's plan for humanity. Instead many Jews wished to distance themselves from the Christian faith which they held accountable for the destruction of six million Jews. For Jewry the death camps came to symbolize the last link in the chain of twenty centuries of anti-Semitism. Despite this rift, several Jewish theologians were influenced by various aspects of Christian thought in attempting to make religious sense of the events of the Nazi period. The American Jewish theologian Richard Rubenstein for example was profoundly affected by an encounter he had in the 1960s with the Dean of the Evangelical Church in East and West Berlin. Provoked to reformulate his understanding of God, he advanced a mystical theology akin to the religious systems of the East. A very different approach has been undertaken by the American theologian Emil Fackenheim who argued that in Auschwitz God issued the 614th commandment. The divine imperative to resist the forces of modern secularism. he believed, was issued to both Jews and Christians – in his writing he cited the example of a Polish Catholic whose reaction to the Nazis symbolized such resistance. Two other theologians of the contemporary period – Ignaz Maybaum and Arthur Cohen – also struggled to make religious sense of the Nazi onslaught by appealing to Christian theological motifs. In his explanation of God's role in the slaughter of the Jewish people, Maybaum appealed to the themes of Calvary, Golgatha, the suffering servant, and vicarious sacrificial atonement; Cohen on the other hand transformed the concept of the *Mysterium Tremendum* (as found in the work of the Protestant scholar Rudolf Otto) in his discussion of the significance of the Holocaust.

For nearly four millennia then Judaism has in various ways espoused a generally indulgent attitude toward other religions. Unlike the Christian faith which has had a long tradition of Exclusivism, Jews have been encouraged to grant other religions a role in the unfolding of God's purposes. Such Jewish Inclusivism presupposes the superiority of the Jewish faith, however it recognizes that God's purposes have been served by other nations and that he has had an authentic encounter with other peoples. As we have seen, such ideas have been largely confined to a consideration of Christianity, and in some cases Islam. Only occasionally are there references to other religions. Yet there is no denying the Inclusivist thrust of centuries of Jewish teaching: religious tolerance has been the hallmark of Judaism through the ages.

A PLURALISTIC MODEL

Given the largely tolerant attitude of Judaism to other faiths, should Jews move beyond such Inclusivism? As previously noted, the Inclusivist position suffers from serious theological defects: Inclusivists appear to affirm two incompatible convictions – the belief in God's universal concern and the conviction that he has definitively revealed himself to a particular group. Arguably such a position is internally incoherent: if God is truly concerned with the fate of all humanity, he would not have disclosed himself fully and finally to a particular people allowing the rest of humanity to wallow in darkness and ignorance. Rather what is required today is an even more open approach to the world's religions. To use a model of the universe of faiths formulated by the Protestant theologian John Hick, a Copernican Revolution is now required in our understanding of religion. In the past even the most liberal Jewish thinkers retained the conviction that Judaism contains the fullest divine disclosure; while recognizing the inherent value of other religions – particularly Christianity – they were convinced that Judaism is humanity's future hope. These Jewish thinkers were like scientists who previously endorsed a Ptolemaic view of the universe in which the earth is at the centre.

In the modern world however where Jews continually come into contact with adherents of other religious traditions, it is difficult to sustain such a narrow vision. Instead a Copernican Revolution is currently required in our understanding of the universe of faiths. Instead of placing Judaism at the centre of the world's religions, a theocentric model should be adopted – such a transformation demands a paradigm shift from a Judeo-centric to a theo-centric conception of religious history. On this basis, the world's religions should be understood as different human responses to the one divine reality. In previous ages religions conceived of this one reality either theistically (as a personal deity) or non-theistically (as non-personal), but such differences were in essence the result of historical, cultural or psychological influences. This shift from a Judeo-centric to a theo-centric model is represented diagrammatically in Figure 9.1.

On this view there is one ultimate Reality behind all religious expressions. To use kabbalistic terminology, the Godhead is the *Ayn Sof* – the Infinite beyond human comprehension. The Godhead is the eternal Reality which provides the inspiration for all religions including Judaism. This ultimate Reality is interpreted in a variety of different modes, and these different explanations of the one Reality have inevitably given rise to a variety of differing and competing conceptions.

Such a view of the Divine in relation to the world's religions can be represented as well by the image of alternative paths ascending

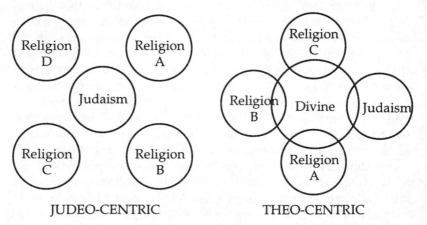

JUDEO-CENTRIC   THEO-CENTRIC

Figure 9.1

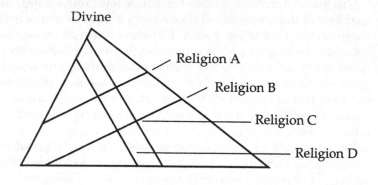

Figure 9.2

a single mountain – each route symbolizes a particular religion with divine Reality floating like a cloud above the mountain top (Figure 9.2).

The routes of these faith communities are all different, yet at various points they intersect: these intersections should be understood at those areas where religious conceptions within the differing traditions complement one another. Thus as pilgrims of different faiths ascend to the summit, they will encounter parallels with their own traditions. But the divine Reality they all pursue is in the end unattainable by these finite quests. As the Infinite, it is unknowable and incomprehensible. It is the cloud of unknowing.

Such a Pluralistic model implies that conceptions of the Divine in the world's religions are ultimately human images – they represent the myriad ways of approaching the one indescribably divine Reality. Doctrinal differences (such as the Judeo-Christian belief in one life in this world as against the Indian doctrine of reincarnation) reflect differences in the historical, social and cultural factors lying behind these convictions. Not only does this Pluralistic framework offer a more comprehensible theoretical basis for understanding differences between religious systems, it also provides a wider forum for interfaith encounter. Instead of assuming, as Jewish Inclusivists have in the past, that Judaism embodies God's all-embracing truth of which other religions possess only a share, Jewish Pluralism encourages Jews to engage in fruitful and enriching dialogue with members of other traditions.

This new Pluralistic model further reflects our current understanding of the world in which no truth is viewed as unchanging.
Rather truth-claims by their very nature must be open to other
insights. They prove themselves not by triumphing over other
belief systems, but by testing their compatibility with other truths.
Such a conception of relational-truth affords a new orientation to
our understanding of truth in religion; on this view religious truth
is not static but instead undergoes continual interaction and
development.

This model of truth-through-relationship allows each religion to
be unique – the truth it contains is uniquely important for religious
adherents. But it is not true in a universal sense. Religious truth is
relevant only for those who subscribe to it. Judaism thus should not
be conceived as the one, true faith for all human beings as a
number of previous Jewish Inclusivists have argued. Rather,
Judaism is true only for the Jewish people. It might be objected that
such a relativistic conception of religious truth would inevitably
diminish one's commitment as a Jew; however one can be totally
committed to the Jewish faith while at the same time genuinely
open to other religions. Using the analogy of marriage, Paul Knitter
argued that in expressing devotion to one's spouse, one is not
making any kind of universal claim: 'one can be totally and
faithfully committed to one's spouse, even though one well knows
that there are other persons in this world equally as good,
intelligent, beautiful – yes, even when one makes the acquaintance
of and enjoys the friendship of such persons. Absolute exclusivity,
in attitude or practice is neither honest, or healthy in any
commitment.' (Knitter, 1985, 201). Further, Knitter argued that the
deeper the commitment to one's spouse and the more secure the
marriage, the more one can appreciate the truth and beauty of
others – similarly the deeper one's commitment to Judaism, the
greater can be one's openness to other faiths.

A Pluralist confessional stance is thus both certain and open-
ended: it enables Jews to affirm the uniqueness of their faith while
urging them to recognize the validity of other traditions. Jewish
Inclusivism – with its insistence on completeness and finality –
simply does not fit what is being experienced in the arena of
religious diversity. In place of a Judeo-centric conception of God's
activity, divine Reality must be placed at the centre of the universe
of faiths. Within such a context, Judaism can be seen as an
authentic and true religious expression. Here then is a new

framework for positive encounter and religious harmony: if Jews can free themselves from an absolutist standpoint in which claims are viewed as possessing ultimate and universal truth, the way is open for a radically new vision of Jewish dialogue with the world's faiths.

A THEOLOGY OF RELIGIOUS PLURALISM

How is one to account for the plurality of religions given the existence of a divine Reality at the centre of the universe of faiths? Following the Kantain distinction between the world-as-it-is (the noumenal world) and the world as perceived (the phenomenal world), the Real *an sich* (in itself) should be distinguished from the Real as conceived in human thought and experience. Such a contrast is a central feature of many of the world's faiths: thus in Judaism God as the transcendental Infinite is conceived as *Ayn Sof* as distinct from the *Shekinah* (God's Presence) which is manifest in the terrestrial plane; in Hindu thought the *nirguna* Brahman, the Ultimate in itself, beyond all human categories is distinguished from the *saguna* Brahman, the Ultimate as known to finite consciousness as a personal deity, Isvara; in Taoist thought 'the Tao that can be expressed is not the eternal Tao'; in Mahayana Buddhism there is a contrast between the eternal cosmic Buddha-nature, which is also the infinite Void and on the other hand the realm of the heavenly Buddha figures in and their incarnations in the earthly Buddhas.

In attempting to represent ultimate reality the different religions have conceptualized the Divine in two distinct modes: the Real personalized and the Real as Absolute. In the Christian faith God is understood as Father; in Judaism as Lord; in Islam as Allah; in the Indian traditions as Shiva, or Vishnu, or Parameter. In each case these personal deities are conceived as acting within the history of the various faith communities. Thus as John Hick explained with regard to Yahweh in the Jewish tradition and Shiva in Hinduism:

> The Yahweh *persona* exists and has developed in interaction with the Jewish people. He is a part of their history, and they are a part of his; and he cannot be extracted from this historical context. Shiva, on the other hand, is a quite different divine *persona* existing in the experience of hundreds of millions of

people in the Shaivite stream of Indian religious life. These two *personae*, Yahweh and Shiva live within different worlds of faith, partly creating and partly created by the features of different human cultures.... From a pluralist point of view *Yahweh* and Shiva are not rival gods, or rival claimants to be the one and only God, but rather two different concrete historical *personae* in terms of which the ultimate divine Reality is present and responded to by different large historical communities within different strands of the human story.

(Hick, 1985, 42)

The concept of the Absolute is alternatively schematized to form a range of divine conceptualizations in the world's religions such as Brahman, the Dharma, the Tao, Nirvana, Sunyata in Eastern traditions. Unlike divine *personae* which are concrete and often visualized, divine *impersonae* constitute a variety of concepts such as the infinite being-consciousness-bliss of Brahman, the beginningless and endless of cosmic change of Buddhist teachings, the ineffable further shore of Nirvana, the eternal Buddha-nature or the ultimate Emptiness which is also the fullness of the world, and the eternal principle of the Tao. These non-personal representations of the Divine inform modes of consciousness ranging from the experience of becoming one with the Infinite to finding total reality in a concrete historical moment of existence.

Given the diversity of images of the Real among the various religious systems that have emerged throughout history, it is not surprising that there are innumerable conflicts between the teachings of the world's faiths – in all cases believers have maintained that the doctrines of these respective traditions are true and superior to competing claims. Thus Jews contend that they are God's chosen people and partners in a special covenant – their mission is to be a light to the nations. In this sense the Jewish people stand in a unique relationship with God. This does not lead to the quest to convert others to Judaism, but it does give rise to a sense of pride in having been born into the Jewish fold.

With Islam, Muslims are convinced that Muhammad was the seal of the prophets and that through the Qur'an God revealed himself decisively to the world. This implies that while Muslims are obligated to recognize the veracity of the other Abrahamic traditions – and in some cases extend the Qur'anic concept of the People of the Book to other faiths as well – they nonetheless assert that the

Qur'an has a unique status as God's final, decisive word. Similarly Christians affirm the unique superiority of the Christian faith since Jesus Christ was God himself, the second person of the Trinity in human form. On the basis of this central dogma, they view themselves as the heirs of the one and only true religion. Convinced that only those who belong to the true faith could be saved, the Christian community has throughout history sought to convert all human beings to the Gospel.

Hindus on the other hand believe that it is possible to have access to eternal truth as incarnated in human language in the Vedas. Although Hindus are tolerant of other faiths, it is assumed that in this life or in the life to come all will come to the fullness of Vedic understanding. Further, in advaitic philosophy it is maintained that the theistic forms of religion embody an inferior conception of ultimate Reality. Thus Hindus believe that their faith is uniquely superior to other religious conceptions. Likewise in the Buddhist tradition, it is assumed that the true understanding of the human condition is presented in the teachings of Gautama Buddha. The Dharma, Buddhists stress, contains the full and saving truth for all humanity.

Each of these religious traditions then affirms its own superiority – all rival claims are regarded as misapprehensions of ultimate Reality. From a Pluralistic perspective however there is no way to ascertain which, if any, of these spiritual paths accurately reflects the nature of the Real *an sich*. In the end, the varied truth-claims of the world's faiths must be regarded as human images which are constructed from within particular social and cultural contexts. Hence from a Pluralistic perspective it is impossible to make judgements about the veracity of the various conceptions of the Divine within the world's faiths. Thus neither Jew, Muslim, Christian, Hindu nor Buddhist has any justification for believing that his respective tradition embodies the uniquely true and superior religious path – instead the adherents of all the world's faiths must recognize the inevitably human subjectivity of religious conceptualization. A theology of religious Pluralism thus calls for a complete reorientation of religious apprehension. What is now required is for all believers to acknowledge that their conceptual systems, forms of worship, life styles and Scriptures are in the end nothing more than lenses through which different communities perceive Reality. But the Divine as-it-is-in-itself is beyond human understanding.

RANKING JUDAISM AND OTHER FAITHS

Assuming that divine Reality, rather than the Jewish tradition, is at the centre of the universe of faiths, does such a Pluralistic model of the world's religions imply that all religions are equally valid? Within Jewish circles there has been no discussion of this issue; however in the Christian world a number of Pluralist theologians have begun to explore this topic. John Hick for example has asserted that religious concepts are not all on the same level of value or validity. This is so among the different religions and even within individual religious systems. Indeed, throughout history the most significant religious figures have been critical of various ideas and attitudes: Gautama rejected the notion of the eternal *atman*; the Hebrew prophets criticized mere outward observances and practices; Jesus attacked the formalism and insincerity of the scribes and Pharisees; Muhammad rejected the polytheism of Arabian society; Guru Nanak and Martin Luther were critical of the traditions into which they were born. Thus Hick maintained that assessing religious phenomena is a central feature of religious seriousness and openness to the Divine.

It is legitimate, he continued, to grade aspects of religions and place them in some order of merit. No one is going to think that all the features of the world's religions are on the same level of value or validity; different aspects have to be regarded as higher or lower, better or worse, Divine or demonic.' (Hick, 1981, 451). Yet Hick was anxious to emphasize that while it is proper to assess religious phenomena, it is not realistic to grade the world's religions as totalities. 'Each of these long traditions,' he wrote, 'is so internally diverse, containing so many different kinds of both good and evil, that it is impossible for human judgement to weigh up and compare their merits as systems of salvation.' (Hick, 1981, 467). Commenting on this view, Paul Griffiths and Delmas Lewis described Hick as a non-judgemental Inclusivist who is unwilling to make judgements about the claims of the world's religions, (Griffiths and Lewis, 1983, 75–80), but this is a mistake. Hick has made it clear throughout his discussion that it is the theologian's proper task to ascertain what aspects of a tradition are 'belief-worthy, revelatory, plausible, rightly claiming allegiance'. (Hick, 1981, 457).

The difficulty with Hick's position is not, as Griffith and Lewis claimed, that he has refused to make judgements about the truth-claims of religions, but rather that the evaluative framework he outlined is open to serious criticism. The first criterion Hick proposed is theological coherence: 'We can try to assess such a system in respect of its internal consistency...' (Hicks, 1981, 462). Yet there is no self-evident reason why internal consistency should necessarily be regarded as a central virtue of a religion. It may well be that religious experience transcends ordinary categories of logical reasoning; furthermore even if it were shown that a religious system is coherent in terms of belief and practice, this would not necessarily imply that it was in fact based on a true encounter with divine Reality. Allied with this notion of internal coherence is a second criterion of religious adequacy – 'its adequacy both to the particular form of experience on which it is based and to the data of human experience in general'. (Hick, 1981, 462). Here, however, it is unclear how one is to determine whether a theology or philosophy within a religious tradition is adequate to the originating religious vision or successful in interpreting that vision to a new age. There is no doubt that the theologies of Thomas Aquinas, al-Ghazali, Maimonides, Shankara and Buddhagohosha are intellectually impressive, but are they true to the original vision on which they are based? Are they successful interpretations for subsequent believers? There is no obvious way to deal with these questions, and any answers will inevitably be based on subjective reactions and interpretations.

The third criterion Hick suggested is spiritual in nature. Here the test consists in ascertaining the extent to which religious ideas promote or hinder the aims of salvation or liberation. 'And by salvation or liberation.' Hick wrote, 'I suggest that we should mean the realization of that limitlessly better quality of human existence which comes about in the transition from self-centredness to Reality-centredness.' (Hick, 1981, 467). In explaining this principle Hick gave examples from several religions: Christians give themselves to God in Christ in a total renunciation of the self-centred ego and its concerns; Muslims give themselves in total submission to God; Hindus strive for union with the Ultimate through meditation and selfless action. While it is true that within the world's religions this theme of selflessness in different forms is an important feature, there are other central motifs as well. Whether this aspect should be the touchstone of religious validity is open to debate. Religious systems provide different and varied spiritual fruits – it is certainly plausible that other spiritual attitudes and concerns are of equal or even superior value than ego-renunciation and self-giving to the Real.

The final criterion Hick proposed is moral assessment. In recommending this standard Hick extolled the lives of various saints of the world's religions, yet he emphasized that the actual histories of religious traditions frequently fall short of moral ideals. In this context he catalogued that he considers modern moral evils engendered by religious faith. In making these judgements Hick wished to illustrate that in the history of all religious traditions there is both virtue and vice. Nevertheless, what is absent from this list is a systematic framework for ethical decision-making. Moral attitudes are notoriously difficult to assess. Does Hick recommend we adopt a teleological or deontological stance? When considering the viability of religious claims concerning the multifarious dimensions of human behaviour, what is to be the basis for making a correct judgement? These central questions are unfortunately left unanswered despite Hick's assurances that certain aspects of the world's faiths are morally inadequate, thereby rendering them religiously less viable.

Similar criticisms made of Hick's criteria can be levelled at the bases for grading religious faiths delineated by Paul Knitter. There are, he maintained, three guidelines for determining the truth-value of any religion or religious figure: (1) Personally, does the revelation of the religion or religious figure – the story, the myth, the message – move the human heart? Does it stir one's feelings, the depths of one's horizons? (2) Practically, does the message provide for psychological health of individuals, their sense of value, purpose and freedom? (Knitter, 1985, 231). As in the case of Hick's criteria, the answers to these questions will inevitably involve subjective interpretation and personal judgement. For example, the life and teachings of Jesus evoke a spiritual response on the part of Christians but have little meaning for Jews. Similarly, the Buddha is of profound significance for Buddhists but has little relevance for Muslims. Again, the legal system of Islam has no significance for Hindus. In all these cases, it is simply impossible to make an objective evaluation of the truth claims of the world's religions on the basis of an existential response. The same applies to the intellectual coherence of religious traditions: Jews, for example, find the Christian doctrines of the Trinity and Incarnation irrational and incoherent. For Christians the Theravada Buddhist's rejection of a supernatural deity undermines the spiritual life. Muslims regard

Hindu polytheism as religiously abhorrent. Thus, Knitter's second criterion also fails to provide a firm foundation for evaluative judgement. The third criterion is equally problematic: how is one to assess whether particular religious beliefs promote psychological health and liberation? Orthodox adherents, for example (such as Orthodox Jews, Roman Catholics and fundamentalist Muslims) regard liberal movements within their own faiths as misguided; liberals on the other hand argue that certain traditional elements of their faiths are psychologically constraining and hinder personal and communal growth. We can see therefore that Knitter's suggestions, like Hick's, fall short of providing a satisfactory basis for ranking religions.

These proposals for evaluating religions are ultimately unsatisfactory because they fail to provide clear-cut and generally accepted bases for evaluation. Yet this should not be a surprising conclusion. In the past adherents of a particular religion judged all other religions by the criteria of their own faith; the eclipse of such an Exclusivist stance by a Pluralistic picture of the world's religions inevitably leads to a relativistic conception of the universe of faiths. Within such a framework grading religions – whether on the basis of theological coherence, religious adequacy, spirituality, morality, existential response, psychological health, or liberating capacity – involves subjective, personal decisions grounded on fundamental presuppositions above divine Reality and the human condition. Given such a situation, claims about religious superiority should be abandoned. Instead the adherents of all faiths should regard one another with respect, acknowledging the spiritual validity of one another's traditions. As far as Judaism is concerned, the Pluralistic model of the world's religions provides a framework for understanding Judaism within the context of the human spiritual quest. Rather than proclaiming the superiority of the Jewish faith, Jewry should acknowledge the integrity of all the world's faiths – Christianity, Islam, Hinduism, Buddhism, Confucianism, Sikhism, Janism, Parsi, as well as the new religions of the modern age.

THEOLOGICAL IMPLICATIONS OF JEWISH PLURALISM

For over two thousand years Jews have daily recited the *Shema*: 'Hear O Israel: the Lord our God is one Lord' (Deuteronomy 6:4). Jewish children are taught this verse as soon as they can speak, and it is recited at their deathbed. Jewish martyrs proclaimed these words as they gave up their lives. Throughout the ages it has been the most important declaration in the Jewish faith. In making this statement Jews, whether Exclusivist or Inclusivist in orientation, attest to their belief that there is only one God and that he is indivisible. He is an absolute unity who cannot be syncretistically linked with other gods. In addition, since the word 'one' in Hebrew also means 'unique', Jews imply that God is different from anything else that is worshipped; only he possesses divinity. Nothing can be compared to him: 'To whom then will ye liken me that I should be equal' (Isaiah 40:25). Thus Jewish monotheism denies the existence of any other divine being; there is only one supreme being who is Lord of all.

Within a Pluralist framework, however, such absolute claims about God should be understood as human conceptions stemming from the religious experience of the ancient Israelites as well as later generations of Jewish sages: Jewish monotheism – embracing a myriad of formulations from biblical through medieval and modern times – is rooted in the life of the people. In all cases pious believers and thinkers have expressed their understanding of God's activity on the basis of their own personal as well as communal encounter with the Divine. Yet given that the Real *an sich* is beyond human comprehension, this Jewish understanding of the Godhead cannot be viewed as definitive and final. Rather, it must be seen as only one among many ways in which human beings have attempted to make sense of the Ultimate. In this light, it makes no sense for Jews to believe that they possess the unique truth about God and his action in the world; on the contrary, universalistic truth-claims about divine Reality must give way to a recognition of the inevitable subjectivity of beliefs about the Real.

The same conclusion applies to the Jewish belief about God's revelation. According to tradition, the Hebrew Scriptures were communicated by God to the Jewish people. In Maimonides' formulation of the thirteen principles of the Jewish faith, this belief is a central tenet: 'The Torah was revealed from heaven. This implies our belief that the whole of the Torah found in our hands this day is the Torah that was handed down by Moses and that it is all of divine origin.' Further, the rabbis maintained that the expositions and elaborations of the Written law contained in the Torah were also revealed by God to Moses on Mount Sinai; subsequently they were passed on from generation to generation and through this process additional legislation was incorporated. Thus traditional Judaism affirms that God's revelation is twofold and binding for all time.

A theory of Jewish Pluralism however calls such convictions into question. Instead of affirming that God uniquely disclosed his word to the Jewish people in Scripture and through the teachings of the sages, Jews should acknowledge that their Holy Writ is only one record of divine communication among many. Both the Written and the Oral Torah have special significance for the Jewish people, but this does not imply that these writings contain a uniquely true and superior divine communication. Instead the *Tanakh* and rabbinic literature should be perceived as a record of the spiritual life of the people and a testimony of their religious quest; as such they should be viewed in much the same light as the New Testament, the Qur'an, the Bagahavad Gita, the Vedas and so forth. For the Jewish people this sacred literature has particular meaning – yet it should not be regarded as possessing ultimate truth.

Likewise the doctrine of the chosen people must be revised from a Pluralistic viewpoint. Throughout history the belief that Israel is God's chosen people has been a central feature of the tradition. Through its election, Jewry believed it had been given an historic mission to bear divine truth to humanity. God's choice of Israel thus carries with it numerous responsibilities: Israel is obligated to keep God's statutes and observe his laws, and in doing so, the nation will be able to persuade others that there is only one universal God. By carrying out this task, Israel is to be a light to the nations.

Here again, Jewish Pluralism must draw attention to the inevitable subjectivity of these claims about Israel's relationship with God and its universal role in a divine providential plan. Although Jews have derived great strength from such convictions, they are based on a misapprehension of Judaism in the context of the universe of faiths. Given that the Real *an sich* transcends human understanding, the conviction that God has selected a particular people as his agent is nothing more than an expression of the Jewish people's sense of superiority and impulse to spread its religious message. In fact however there is simply no way of knowing if a specific people stands in a special relationship with the Divine.

Again, a Pluralistic approach challenges the traditional Jewish conviction that God has a providential plan for the Jewish people and for all humankind. The Bible asserts that God controls and guides the universe – such a view implies that the manifestation of a wise and benevolent providence is found everywhere. Subsequently the doctrine of divine providence was developed in rabbinic literature, and the belief that God is concerned with each individual as well as the world in general became a central feature of Jewish theology.

From a Pluralistic perspective however such a religious conviction must be seen as simply one way of interpreting Reality. The belief that God's guiding hand is manifest in all things is ultimately a human response to the universe – it is not, as Jews have believed through the ages, certain knowledge. This is illustrated by the fact that other traditions have postulated a similar view of providence, yet maintain that God's action in history (as for example in the case of Jesus's passion or the growth and development of Islam) has taken an entirely different form. In other cases non-theistic religions have formulated conceptions of human destiny divorced from the activity of God or the gods. Such differences in interpretation highlight the subjectivity of all these beliefs.

The Jewish doctrine of the Messiah must also be seen in a similar light from a Pluralist perspective. Throughout history the Jewish people longed for a messianic figure who would redeem the nation from exile and inaugurate a period of peace and harmony. According to tradition, the messianic age will last for a millennium and will be followed by a final judgement in which the righteous will be rewarded and the wicked punished. For two millennia Jews have waited patiently for the coming of the Messiah and daily pray for his arrival.

Within a Pluralist framework such longing must be perceived as a pious hope based on personal and communal expectation. Although this belief has served as a bedrock of the Jewish faith through the centuries, it is inevitably shaped by human conceptualization. Like other doctrines in the Jewish tradition, it has been grounded in the experience of the Jewish people and has undergone a range of changes in the history of the nation. Because the Real *an sich* is beyond comprehension, there is simply no way of ascertaining whether this belief in a personal Messiah accurately mirrors the nature of ultimate Reality.

Finally Jewish Pluralism demands a similar stance regarding the doctrine of the Afterlife. Although the Bible does not contain an elaborate doctrine of the Hereafter, the rabbis developed a complex eschatological picture of human history. According to tradition, the World-to-Come is divided into several stages: first, there is the time of messianic redemption. Peace will reign throughout nature; Jerusalem will be rebuilt and at the close of this era, the dead will be resurrected and rejoined with their souls. Final judgement will then come upon all. Those who are judged righteous will enter into Heaven, and the wicked will be punished in Hell.

While this set of beliefs regarding the eschatological unfolding of history has been a central feature of the Jewish faith from rabbinic times to the present, it is simply impossible to ascertain whether these events will unfold in the future. In our finite world – limited by space and time – certain knowledge about life after death is unobtainable. Belief in the hereafter in which the righteous of Israel will receive their just reward has sustained the nation through suffering and tragedy, yet from a Pluralistic outlook these doctrines are no more certain that any other features of the Jewish religious heritage.

The implications of such a Copernican shift from Inclusivism to Pluralism are radical and far-reaching. Judaism, like all other religions, advances absolute, universal truth-claims about the nature of Reality – but given the separation between our finite understanding and the Real *an sich*, there is no way of attaining complete certitude about the veracity of these beliefs. The Real transcends human comprehension, and hence it must be admitted that Jewish religious convictions are no different in principle from those found in other religious traditions – all are lenses through which divine reality is conceptualized. Judaism, like all other major world religions, is built around its one distinctive way of thinking and experiencing the Divine, yet in the end the Jewish Pluralist must remain agnostic about the correctness of his own religious convictions.

Conclusion

This survey of Jewish attitudes to other faiths over the centuries reveals the generally tolerant orientation of the tradition. In ancient Israel foreign gods were viewed as non-entities; nonetheless pagans were not condemned for their religious beliefs and practices – idolatry was considered sinful only for the Israelite nation. This attitude was elaborated by rabbinic scholars who maintained that even those who worship idols are acceptable to God as long as their worship of idols points to the one true Lord. Later this notion of symbolic intermediacy was applied by such medieval scholars as Rabbenu Tam to Christianity. In his view, the Christian faith – despite its adherence to the doctrine of the Trinity – is monotheistic. Other writers of the period such as Judah Halevi advocated an even more tolerant form of Inclusivism in which Christians and Muslims were perceived as having an important role in the unfolding of God's providential scheme.

Despite the persecution and massacre of Jewry that took place during the Middle Ages, this spirit of acceptance continued into the early modern period. With the dawn of the Enlightenment Jewish thinkers such as Moses Mendelssohn, Joseph Salvador and Abraham Geiger advanced a similarly appreciative interpretation of Christianity. Other scholars such as Samuel Hirsch, Solomon Formstecher, Solomon Steinheim, and Claude Montefiore were likewise concerned to view the Christian faith in a positive light. This approach was subsequently further developed by Max Bord, Franz Rosenzweig, Leo Baeck, Martin Buber, and Jacob Klausner. Although the Holocaust eclipsed this positive assessment of Christianity, a number of contemporary writers – including Richard Rubenstein, Emil Fackenheim, Ignaz Maybaum, and Arthur A. Cohen – have been deeply influenced by Christian ideas and motifs in attempting to make sense of God's dealings with the Jewish people during the Nazi era.

From this overview it is evident that Jewish thinkers through the ages have in different ways affirmed that monotheistic traditions should be regarded as religiously acceptable. Among the writers surveyed the dominant attitude has been a Jewish form of Inclusivism. For these writers Judaism is the ultimately true faith, yet other religions – especially Christianity and Islam – have been regarded as playing an important role in the unfolding of God's eschatological plan. In the contemporary world however the Jewish community needs to adopt an even more open stance towards the world's religions. What is required today is a shift from Inclusivism to Pluralism in which the Divine – rather than Judaism – is placed at the centre of the universe of faiths. Such Pluralism would enable Jews to affirm the uniqueness of Judaism while acknowledging the religious validity of other religions. The theology underpinning this shift in perspective is based on the distinction between the Real *an sich* and the Real as perceived. From this vantage point, the truth-claims of all religions should be regarded as human constructions rather than universally valid doctrines.

Given the shift from Jewish Inclusivism to Jewish Pluralism, the way is now open to interfaith encounter on the deepest level. Preeminent among areas in which Jewish Pluralists can participate with members of other religions is the sphere of prayer. No longer should Jews feel constrained to stand aloof from attending the worship services of other faiths or participating in joint prayer. Rather a Pluralist standpoint in which all faiths are recognized as authentic paths to ultimate Reality would encourage adherents of all the world's religions – including Jewry – to engage in common religious activities. In this regard it is important to distinguish between three major types of interfaith worship:

1. Services of a particular religious community in which adherents of other faiths are invited as guests. On such occasions, it is customary to ask a representative of the visiting faith – community to recite a suitable prayer or preach a sermon, but the liturgy remains the same.
2. Interfaith gatherings of a serial nature. At such meetings representatives of each religious community offer prayers or readings usually on a common theme. Those present constitute an audience listening to a liturgical anthology in which the distinctiveness of each religion is recognized, but everyone is free to participate as well.
3. Interfaith gatherings with a common order of service. In such situations all present are participants and there is an overarching theme. Possibly a unifying symbol – such as the lighting of candles – is used. A typical example of such a service is the annual multi-faith observance for Commonwealth Day when the following prayer is recited:

We affirm our common faith in the dignity and unique worth of the human person, independent of colour, class or creed. We affirm our common faith in the need to establish justice between man and man, and, through common effort, to secure peace and reconciliation between nations. We affirm our common faith in the need to assert the supremacy of love in all human relationships. We affirm our common faith in the brotherhood of man and our concern to express it in service and sacrifice for the common weal.

(Braybrooke, 1992, 152)

These various services possess their own particular characteristics. In the first type of service – when adherents of one faith invite others to attend their services – they are not setting out to make converts; rather, there is a conscious recognition of the integrity of other traditions. In such a gathering Jewish Pluralists should feel completely comfortable: a Pluralist outlook would encourage the process of learning and sharing, and ideally Jewish guests at another faith-community's worship service should strive to enter into the religious experience of those praying. In this regard Jewish Pluralists should not feel constrained reciting prayers or singing hymns whose truth-claims contradict the truth-claims of their own faith. Given that the Real *an sich* is unknowable, the various liturgical formulations in the world's faiths should be understood as human constructions which attempt to depict the nature and activity of a divine Reality – as models of the Divine, they guide the believer to the Ultimate. From this perspective, Jewish Pluralists should have no hesitation in joining with Christians, Muslims, Buddhists, Hindus, Sikhs, as well as adherents of all the world's religions in the recitation of their respective liturgies.

Similarly in the second type of worship service – in which there is a serial reading from representatives of other communities – Jewish Pluralists ought to welcome the opportunity to share their liturgical tradition with others and should feel no reluctance in joining in the liturgy from other traditions when appropriate. In accord with a Pluralist stance, such serial services are based on mutual respect and afford each faith community an equal role in worship. Frequently such gatherings take place in order to affirm the common humanity of all the world's faiths – this for example has been the basis of the World Day of Prayer for Peace at Assisi. Jewish Pluralism would embrace and encourage such initiatives.

Turning to the third type of worship service – in which there is a shared liturgy – Jewish Pluralists can be open to the opportunity to pray together in this way with members of other faiths. In such contexts participants are frequently invited to worship the One Eternal One – the ultimate ground of being to which all religious dogma and ritual point as the Divine Mystery. This form of service is particularly amenable to a Pluralist theology in which final Reality is conceived as the unknowable Infinite that cannot be fully expressed in any particular faith. In services of this type the distinctiveness of each religion is accepted – there is no attempt to replace the regular liturgy and prayer of the individual faith communities. Yet there is the implicit assumption that in worship the adherents of all faiths stand before the Ultimate to which they have given different names. As the universal prayer from the Week for World Peace proclaims:

> O God of many names. Lover of all nations, we pray for peace: in our hearts, in our homes, in our nations, in our world. The peace of your will.
>
> (Braybrooke, 1992, 151)

The third form of worship then is consonant with the principles of Jewish Pluralism – it affirms other faiths while at the same time recognizing the limitation of all human conceptualizations of the Real.

A second area in which Jewish Pluralists are able to join members of other faiths is the sphere of theological exploration. In the past Jewish theologians insisted that Judaism is the superior faith – even the most liberal Inclusivists maintained that in the future all human beings will recognize the truth of Jewish monotheism. In this sense Jewish theology throughout the centuries was Judeocentric in character. Today in our religiously diverse world however it is no longer possible to sustain this view – what is required instead is a complete redefinition of the theological task. In the modern world Jewish thinkers must recognize that theology can no longer be practiced only within a single tradition. The pursuit of religious truth calls for a dialogical approach in a global context. As Wilfred Cantwell Smith has remarked:

> The time will soon be with us when a theologian who attempts to work out his position unaware that he does so as a member of a world society in which other theologians equally intelligent,

equally devout, equally moral, are Hindus, Buddhists, Muslims and unaware that his readers are likely perhaps to be Buddhists or to have Muslim husbands or Hindu colleagues – such a theologian is as out of date as is one who attempts to construct an intellectual position unaware that Aristotle has thought about the world or that existentialists have raised new orientations, or unaware that the earth is a minor planet in a galaxy that is vast only by terrestrial standards.

(Smith, 1962, 123)

The formulation of a Jewish global, interreligious theology hinges on two major preconditions. First, Jewish theologians must learn about other faiths than their own. Jewish global theology requires religious thinkers to explore what the world's faiths have experienced and said about the nature of divine Reality, the phenomenon of religious experience, the nature of the self, the problem of the human condition, and the value of the world. Second, Jewish theologians should attempt to enter as best they can into the thought-world as well as religious experiences of those of other faiths: this can only be done by becoming an active participant in their way of life. As Paul Knitter argued, 'Theologians must "pass over" to the experience, to the mode of being in the world, that furthers the creeds and codes and cults of other religions...[they] must imaginatively participate in the faith of other religions: "Faith can only be theologized from the inside"' (Knitter, 1985, 226). Jewish thinkers must thus enter into the subjectivity of other traditions and bring the resulting insights to bear on their own religious understanding: such theological reflection calls for a multi-dimensional, cross-cultural, inter-religious consciousness. Jewish Pluralism is most suited to such a multi-faceted approach in which all religions are conceived as interdependently significant. Given the quest for a global perspective, Jewish Pluralists must insist that the theological endeavour occurs in a trans-religious context. This enterprise calls for a religious encounter in which Jews confront others who hold totally different truth-claims – such individuals can help Jewish thinkers to discover their own presuppositions and underlying principles. In this process the Jewish partner should be able to recognize the limitations of his own tradition, and as a result make a conscious effort to discover common ground with other faiths. Such an interchange is vital to the elaboration of a multi-dimensional, theological outlook.

On the threshold of the third millennium then Judaism stands on the verge of a new awakening. Drawing on centuries of tolerance the way is now open for Jews to formulate a complete reorientation of the Jewish faith in relation to other religious traditions. With a shift from Inclusivism to Pluralism, there is no longer any need to interpret other religions from a Judeo-centric standpoint, rather with the Divine at the centre of the universe of faiths, Jewry can acknowledge the inevitable subjectivity of all religious beliefs, including those contained in the Jewish heritage. Jewish Pluralism thus demands the recognition that all religions constitute separate paths to divine Reality – yet at the summit of this ascent, the Real *an sich* remains beyond human comprehension: it is the cloud of unknowing beyond human grasp. As the *Shekinah* led the children of Israel for forty years through the wilderness – always present, always ahead, and always unreachable, so the Divine hovers just beyond the range of human apprehension. If the Jewish people are to remain faithful to the age-old vision of the Word of the Lord going forth from Zion, they must listen to that Word as it comes from many Zions, from Mecca as well as Sinai, from Benares as well as Safed, from Rome as well as Vilna, from Kyoto as well as Jerusalem.

Bibliography

Acosta, Uriel, *A Specimen of Human Life*, New York, 1967.

Baeck, Leo, *Judaism and Christianity*, Philadelphia, 1958.

Baeck, Leo, 'Judaism in the Church', *Hebrew College Annual*, 1925.

Baeck, Leo, 'Some Questions to the Christian Church from the Jewish Point of View', *The Church and The Jewish People*, ed. Göte Hedenquist, London, 1954.

Baeck, Leo *The Essence of Judaism*, New York, 1948.

Barth, Karl, Church Dogmatics, vols 1 and 2, Edinburgh, 1956.

Brod, Max, *Der Meister*, Gütersloh, 1952.

Brod, Max, *Heidentum, Christentum, Judentum, ein Bekenntnisbuch*, Munich, 1922.

Brunner, Emil, *Revelation and Reason*, London, 1947.

Buber, Martin, *Die Stunde und die Erkenntnis*, Berlin, 1936.

Buber, Martin, *Israel and the World*, New York, 1948.

Buber, Martin, *The Origin and Meaning of Hasidism*, New York, 1960.

Buber, Martin, *Two Types of Faith*, New York, 1961.

Cohen, Arthur A., *The Tremendum*, New York, 1981.

Cohen, Hermann, *Die Religion der Vernunft aus den Quellen des Judentums*, Berlin, 1911.

Cohen, Hermann, *Jüdische Schriften*, Berlin, 1924.

Cohn-Sherbok, Dan, *Holocaust Theology*, London 1969.

Cohn-Sherbok, Dan, *Issues in Contemporary Judaism*, London, 1991.

Cohn-Sherbok, Dan, *The Crucified Jew: Twenty Centuries of Christian Anti-Semitism*, London, 1992.

Cohn-Sherbok, Dan, *The Jewish Heritage*, Oxford, 1987.

Denzinger, *Enchiridion Symbolorum Definitionum et Declarationum de Rebus Fidei et Morum*, 29th edn, Freiburg, 1952, No. 714.

Da Costa, Gavin, 'Christianity and Other Religions', in Cohn-Sherbok, Dan. (ed.), *Many Mansions*, New York, 1992.

Fackenheim, Emil, *God's Presence in History*, New York, 1972.

Fackenheim, Emil, *Encounters between Judaism and Modern Philosophy* , 1973.

Fackenheim, Emil, *To Mend the World*, New York, 1982.

Formstecher, Solomon, *Die Religion des Geistes*, Frankfurt, 1841.

Geiger, Abraham, *Das Judentum und seine Geschichte*, Breslau, 1910.

Geiger, Abraham, 'Einleitung in das Stadium der jüdische Theologie' *Nachgelassene Schriften*, ed. Ludwig Geigen, Berlin, 1875.

Geiger, Abraham, 'Enstlehung des Christentums', *Jüdische Zeitschrift fur Wissenschaft und Leben* 11, 1874.

Geiger, Abraham, *Judaism and its History*, New York, 1911.

Griffiths, Paul and Lewis, Delmas, 'On Grading Religions, Seeking Truth and Being Nice to People – A Reply to Professor Hick', *Religious Studies*, 1983.

Halbencruetz, C., *Dialogue and Community*, World Council of Churches, 1977.

Halevi, Judah, *Kuzari* in *Three Jewish Philosophers*, New York, 1965.

Hartman, David, 'On the Possibilities of Religious Pluralism from a Jewish Point of View', *Immanuel*, 1983.

Hartman, David, *Conflicting Visions*, New York, 1990.

Hick, John, *God and the Universe of Faiths*, New York, 1973; London, 1977.

Hick, John, *God Has Many Names*, London, 1980.

Hick, John, 'On Grading Religions', *Religious Studies*, London, 1981.

Hick, John, *Problems in Religious Pluralism*, London, 1985.

Hirsch, Samuel, *Die Humanitat als Religion*, Trier, 1854.

Hirsch, Samuel, *Die Religions philosophie der Juden*, Leipzig, 1842.

Jacob, Walter, *Christianity Through Jewish Eyes*, Cincinnati, 1974.

Jacobs, Louis, *A Jewish Theology*, New York, 1973.

Kaufman, Yeheziel, *The Religion of Israel*, 1960.

Klausner, Jacob, *Jesus of Nazareth: His Life, Times, and Teaching*, 1964.

Knitter, Paul, *No Other Name*, New York, 1985.

Kung, H., 'The World Religions in God's Plan of Salvation' in Neuner, J. (ed.), *Christian Revelation and World Religions*, London, 1967.

Maccoby, Hyam, *Judaism on Trial*, London, 1982.

Maimonides, *Commentary on the Mishnah*: 'Abodah Zarah 1.3, Hebrew trans. Y. Kafih, 1965.

Maimonides, *Sefer Ha-Mitzvot*, pos. No. 9., ed. Heller, 1946.

Maimonides, *Teshubot Ha-Rambam*, no. 149, ed. Blau, 1960.

Maimonides, *The Guide for the Perplexed*, trans. S. Pines, Chicago, 1963.

Maybaum, Ignaz, *The Face of God After Auschwitz*, Amsterdam, 1965.

Mendelssohn, Moses, *Judaism and Other Writings*, New York, 1969.

Montefiore, Claude, *Liberal Judaism and Hellenism and Other Essays*, London, 1918.

Montefiore, Claude, *Outlines of Liberal Judaism*, London, 1923.

Montefiore, Claude, *Some Elements of the Religious Teaching of Jesus According to the Synoptic Gospels*, London, 1910.

Montefiore, Claude, *The Synoptic Gospels*, London, 1927.

Neuner, J. (ed.), *Christian Revelation and World's Religions*, London, 1967.

Panikaar, Raimundo, *The Unknown Christ of Hinduism*, New York, 1981.

Poliakov, Leon, *The History of Anti-Semitism*, 2 vols, New York and London, 1965–73.

Race, Alan, *Christians and Religious Pluralism*, London, 1983.

Rahner, Karl, *Theological Investigations*, vol. 5, Darton, Longman and Todd, 1966.

Rahner, Karl, *Theological Investigations*, vol. 14, 1976; vol. 16, 1979.

Rosenzweig, Franz, *Briese*, Berlin, 1935.
Rosenzweig, Franz, *Der Stern der Erlösung*, Heidelberg, 1930.
Rubinstein, Richard, *After Auschwitz*, London, 1964, 1992.
Rubinstein, Richard and Roth, John, *Approaches to Auschwitz*, London, 1982.
Salvador, Joseph, *Das Leben Jesu*, Dresden, 1841.
Salvador, Joseph, *Paris, Rome, Jerusalem, on la question religiense au XXe Siècle*, Paris, 1860.
Samartha, Stanley, *Courage for Dialogue*, New York, 1982.
Schoeps, Hans Joachim, *Jewish Christianity: Factional Disputes in the Early Church*, Philadelphia, 1969.
Schoeps, Hans Joachim, *Paul*, Philadelphia, 1961.
Schoeps, Hans Joachim, *The Jewish Christian Argument*, New York, 1963.
Seltzer, Robert, *Jewish People, Jewish Thought*, New York, 1980.
Smith, Wilfred Cantwell, *The Faith of Other Men*, New York, 1962.
Solomon, Norman, *Judaism and World Religion*, London, 1992.
Spinoza, Baruch, *A Theological Political Treatise* in *The Chief Works of Benedict de Spinoza*, vols 1–2, New York, 1951.
Steinheim, Solomon Ludwig, *Die Offenbarung nach dem Lehrbegriff der Synagogue*, Leipzig, 1863.

Index